Studious Drift

Forerunners: Ideas First

Short books of thought-in-process scholarship, where intense analysis, questioning, and speculation take the lead

FROM THE UNIVERSITY OF MINNESOTA PRESS

(Continued on page 88)

Studious Drift
Movements and Protocols for
a Postdigital Education

Tyson E. Lewis and
Peter B. Hyland

University of Minnesota Press
MINNEAPOLIS
LONDON

Portions of chapter 3 previously appeared as "Experiments in E-Study for a Post-Pandemic World," in *Philosophy and Theory in Higher Education* 3, no. 3 (November 2021).

ISBN 978-1-5179-1321-2 (PB)
ISBN 978-1-4529-6708-0 (Ebook)
ISBN 978-1-4529-6812-4 (Manifold)

Published by the University of Minnesota Press, 2022
111 Third Avenue South, Suite 290
Minneapolis, MN 55401–2520
http://www.upress.umn.edu

Available as a Manifold edition at manifold.umn.edu

The University of Minnesota is an equal-opportunity educator and employer.

Contents

Introduction

WITH THE LAUNCH of the digital platform called Studio_D (https://onstead.cvad.unt.edu/studio-d) in the spring of 2020, neither of us could foresee the impact of Covid-19 that was about to unfold. Our project had been developed months in advance of the pandemic with the hopes of getting interdisciplinary teams of scholars from around the world to write short prompts to (a) facilitate reflection on the ways in which e-learning has come to be embedded in any number of online resources, websites, and apps, and (b) to encourage participants to hack into and suspend the educational processes, subject positions, and relationships that e-learning promote. The prompts we received were exciting and provocative, if not perplexing. Some asked participants to deactivate the ubiquitous knowledge clip by subverting its implicit pedagogical assumptions, others opted to neutralize the spectacle of self-promotion known as the selfie by turning the camera toward the decisively unspectacular spaces used to study. Through intentional glitches, "bad" filming/editing, complex games meant to interrupt the economic exchange of information, and processes that slowed down the accelerationism of contemporary education practices, the prompts explored what happens when learning objectives, outcomes, and measures were left idle and a different modality of studious drift was embraced.

As faculty and students implemented such prompts (which we call protocols), it became clear that the exercise was a meditation not simply on the prevalence of e-learning but also on the effects of Covid-19 on the ways in which we experience education. Students suddenly found their lives increasingly dominated by online courses and their social lives mediated by digital technologies. As such, the focus of the experiments on Studio_D took on a newfound urgency and relevance. The limited scope of Studio_D suddenly expanded and became a way to think about what was happening to education in the present lockdown conditions as well as a meditation on possible alternatives that digital education might take in a postpandemic world. How might our digital experiment with Studio_D promote a diversity of educational forms of life that could challenge the increasing predominance of e-learning, especially now that the Covid-19 crisis has expanded and intensified its reach? This book is an attempt to theorize the practice embodied by Studio_D in relation to this larger question, and, in conclusion, we propose a rather startling thesis: that the internet can become a studio for a radically anarchic and pataphysical practice of education, but only if we struggle against the dominance of the metaphysics of learning that continues to colonize the broader expanse of the postdigital world, threatening to reduce educational life to mere economic management.

Beyond The Metaphysics of E-Learning

In the lecture "What is a Creative Act?," Gilles Deleuze (2007) argues that creation is always a resistance against an external threat. By resisting external controls, an internal potentiality is freed up. One might argue that a similar set of assumptions informs many of the current analyses of the university. It is through the co-optation of the university by external forces such as capitalism that prevent it from creatively reconstituting itself. Symptomatic here is the work of figures like Henry Giroux (2007), who argues that the university is in chains that shackle it to corporate power, the military-industrial complex, and right-wing ideology. Likewise, Stanley Aronowitz (2001) argues that the villains undermining the university include conservatives calling for neoliberal austerity measures or administrators and bureaucrats (as villains who have already stormed the gates and sieged the ivory tower for their own purposes) who defund teaching while calling for continual measures of excellence and effectiveness. Certainly Giroux and Aronowitz are more or less correct in their analyses, and it is undoubtably the case that universities have been co-opted by such forces, though we would doubt there was ever a time when such cooptation was not a defining feature of the university (take, for instance, the intimate relationship between the construction of universities and slavery in the United States).

While not wanting to deny the power of the critiques offered by scholars such as Giroux and Aronowitz, the starting point for this book will be somewhat different. Unlike Deleuze (and, by extension, social critics), we want to begin by inquiring into the *internal* forces at work within the university that lend itself to cooptation from the outside. In other words, what is it about the *educational logic* of the university that makes it amenable to regimes of excellence, neoliberal marketization, austerity economics, corporate bureaucracy, and entrepreneurship (see Readings 1997; Giroux and Giroux 2004; Slaughter and Rhoades 2004; Masschelein and Simons 2009; Fabricant and Brier 2016)?

It is our contention that, at its base, the problem stems from the overwhelming hegemonic dominance of the discourse and practice of learning in all sectors of education, from K-12 to our highest institutions. As Gert Biesta (2006) once wrote, this is symptomatic of the "learnification" of society writ large.[1] The fact that learning is an educational logic predicated on measuring outputs and accessing success and failure lends it as a support to economic imperatives (Arsenjuk and Koerner 2009; Lewis 2013, 2017; Ford 2016). Another way of thinking about this is that learning is the economization

---

1. See also Masschelein, Simons, Bröckling, and Pongratz (2007) for a discussion of the rise of the "learning society."

of education where education becomes concerned with planning and calculation. Equal parts risk assessment and evaluation of efficaciousness in the language of productivity come to define all dimensions of what an educational life worth living might look like. This is not to disparage learning as such, but rather to highlight how learning as an *internal* mode of educational organization and practice within universities can and does appeal to broader economic interests, producing synergy between various sectors of social life that culminates in a new form of subjectivity: the life-long learner who must be continually entrepreneurial in order to reskill him or herself according to the needs of a quickly changing knowledge-based economy (Masschelein and Simons 2008).

More so than the aforementioned scholars, we want to make a stronger claim: learning is an educational metaphysics. As Martin Heidegger once defined it, metaphysics "grounds an age, in that through a specific interpretation of what is and through a specific comprehension of truth it gives to that age the basis upon which it is essentially formed" (1977, 115). Today, according to Heidegger, we live in an age where the dominant definition of being (metaphysically speaking) is determined by and through technological enframing. Science is, essentially, the handmaiden of such enframing. In the university, science takes the form of research, which for Heidegger, has certain essential characteristics. For instance, research is "rigorous" insofar as it enframes or secures a specific object-area, and by doing so, secures the representation of the "real." In this manner, the real comes to be divided up into specific representations pertaining to each science, each mapping out, in advance, a set of objects, laws pertaining to these objects, and a set of admissible questions and methods for experimenting on and with these objects. The enframed area of research thus becomes increasingly internally coherent. This self-referential coherence, in turn, produces a sense of objectness that is as natural as it is measurable and predictable. With regards to atomic physics, this coherence grants a privileged place for contingency in its understanding of the "real." Heidegger writes, "Atomic physics admits only of a guaranteeing of an objective coherence that has a statistical character" (172). Note that, for Heidegger, the attempt to understand the real by atomic physics gives way to a statistical analysis or a calculation of probabilities. The real becomes that which is probable or calculable. Giorgio Agamben seems to offer an important amendment to this line of inquiry. For Agamben (2018), contemporary metaphysics concerns itself with radical contingency (of atomic physics) and with a subsequent management of such contingency through probabilistic sciences. In other word, if contingency comes to ground the age through the laws of quantum mechanics, then science takes on the *management* of such contingency through various calculations pertaining to different kinds of objects. The outcome for Agamben is a fundamental erasure of the question of what is real for the question of management of probabilities.

On our interpretation, learnification of society indicates that learning has become the *educational metaphysics* of the scientific age. It reduces education to a set of contingencies in order to govern these contingencies through the generation of evidence capable of making predictions concerning future outcomes. The science of pedagogy becomes a management strategy concerned with inputs and outputs guided by the law of educational excellence, efficacy, and efficiency. This process, in turn, determines the kind of educational life a student will have, what kinds of opportunities they will have access to, and what kinds of debts will have to be paid to achieve certain ends. Hence the dominance of "learning analytics" that merge "large data sets, statistical techniques, and predictive modeling" for "the measurement, collection, analysis and reporting of data about learners in their contexts, for purposes of understanding and optimizing learning and the environments in which it occurs" (cited in Long and Siemens 2011, 34). Thus the collection of learning analytics simultaneously indicates (a) contingencies in the present that (b) must be managed in order to (c) maintain high probability in future success while (d) ensuring that the measurement and assessment of learning is never complete, never finished, and always in need of further verification and accreditation. Whether we are discussing the smallest atomic movements or the life cycles of learning, what is at stake across scalar levels is a metaphysical commitment to management (of the real).

As Siân Bayne and colleagues argue (2020), digital education, e-learning, and ed-tech are more often than not seen as complicit with the economics of learnification. Internet, computers, and enterprise learning management systems (LMSs) all function to capture data in increasingly sophisticated ways, further transforming education into a statistical science. If this is the case, then the recent acceleration of the digitization of the university, especially during the Covid-19 pandemic, is part and parcel of not simply the learnification of the university but also the dominance of learning as an educational metaphysics writ large. At this point it is important to remember Heidegger's diagnosis of technological enframing in relation to computerization. In *Identity and Difference,* Heidegger argues that the "time of calculation," exemplified in the executable functionality of computer algorithms, now "pulls our thinking in all directions" (2002, 41) to the point where thinking itself begins to take on the enframing structure of planning, predicting, and controlling for variables within the given contingencies of a specified research field. Perhaps we might go so far as to say that what Heidegger is diagnosing here is the rise of *computational* subjectivity necessary to survive within a learning society.

More recently, Deleuze (1995b) wrote that digital language indicates a fundamental shift from discipline to control, from monitoring individual bodies to channeling impersonal data flows, from policing spaces to predicting and modulating future possibilities. On our reading, this would mean that digital technologies extend learning outward from the schoolhouse to the virtual learning environment that simultaneously trains subjects to be lifelong learners while also using algorithms to improve assessment, feedback, prediction of success, and surveillance. On the blog *Dario della Crisis,* Agamben seems to pick up on both Heidegger and Deleuze, presenting a scathing critique of the recent trend toward online learning. In his piece titled "Requiem per gli studenti" (2021), Agamben makes the argument that the hasty push toward e-learning not only has put the last remnants of the university at risk but, more importantly, has sacrificed the educational form-of-life he refers to as *studentato,* or "studenthood." For Agamben, students are those who "amano veramente lo studio [truly love to study]." To safeguard study against learning telematics, Agamben urges students to refuse to enroll in such classes (as with the famous autonomist Marxist refusal to work). Likewise, professors ought to refuse to hold their classes online. Given Agamben's concern with study as a unique form of educational life (1995), this warning is predictable. Classrooms are being exchanged for digital environments that do not challenge learning so much as entrench it via the virtualization of control, and in the process, the unique opportunities for small study groups and studious friendships that arise from the intimate discussions of the university seminar are put in jeopardy. If study is a possible mode of educational life, then can we imagine such a life online? Agamben seems to think that this is highly unlikely, given the "spettrale schermo [spectral screen]" that has captured us. The screen separates students from their form of educational life (studenthood), which is embodied, communal, and dependent upon the university as a specific, physical location that fosters forms of studious association. Expanding on Agamben's essential points, we would further add that the underlying worry concerns the ability of the screen to capture and direct attention away from study.[2] In this sense, the screen becomes nothing more than a technological apparatus of learning, separating students from their potentiality for studenthood, and so becomes the apotheosis of the metaphysics of learning that is part and parcel of scientific (and computational) enframing.[3]

The question then becomes: How to suspend the metaphysics of learning that has now become absolutized in the form of online

2. For an overview of Agamben's critique of the screen and a possible educational response, see Vlieghe 2017 and Lewis and Alirezabeigi 2018.

3. As we explore in chapter 2, this separation happens in two ways: summitting or browsing.

classes without necessarily retreating back to the predigital notion of the campus classroom? This book tackles the question of the politics of higher education by (a) critiquing the metaphysics of learning while offering (b) a *pataphysics* of studioing. This pataphysics is not merely an alternative metaphysics but also an impossible educational form of life that emerges when the space and time dedicated to learning are rendered inoperative. As we conceptualize it throughout this book, the pataphysics of studioing consists of several interlocking dimensions, including the virtual space of the studio, the drifting movement of study, and the experimental writing of protocols (that support study). Our claim is that studioing disrupts the connective points between discourses and practice of learning and economy that form the crux of the *internal* education problem facing the university today. We agree with Agamben that the rise to dominance of online education has fundamentally threatened the studious life of students as well as the foundations of the university. And we agree that the refusal to teach and to enroll in such classes is a serious option to consider. At the same time, we want to provide evidence of how university professors, lecturers, artists, designers, and (of course) students acting as pirates can hack into the digital infrastructure of universities to create online studio spaces that promote new modalities of study. As such, while Agamben contends that the screen is *necessarily* a technological apparatus of learning, we would like to suggest a slight shift and propose the possibility of what we call *e-studioing*, or a form of educational life that experiments with the potentiality for online education that is not reducible to a transactional notion of learning economics. The result will be a theory of e-studioing rather than e-learning that takes place in the virtual studio rather than the virtual learning classroom, is composed of unpractical practices of studying rather than the practicalities of learning, and is supported by the experimental writing of the "scyborg" (la paperson 2017) rather than the learning management strategies of the professor. This is not to suggest some kind of technophilic or neoliberal consumerist fantasy of a techno-corporate future wherein digital devices will "save" the university and "improve" education by making it more excellent, more flexible, more economic, and more accommodating (Horn and Staker 2014). Deleuze and Agamben (not to mention Heidegger) have already warned us of the dangers of such a fantasy. There are no technological fixes for the on-going plight(s) of the university as we have come to know it in the industrialized West. At the same time, we see digitization as a terrain of struggle that should not be villainized or romanticized but rather hacked into and tinkered with in order to produce inefficient, less economic, less optimal, and more entropic/anarchic forms of pataphysical life that might very well seem absurd and unprofessional through the looking glass of the metaphysics of learning. Indeed, if we are truly living in a postdigital world in which divisions between online and offline educational environments are increasingly blurred (Ryberg 2021), then thinking the university without also thinking about the educational implications of digital technologies has ceased to make sense. We cannot, as Agamben seems to suggest, screen out the screen. Indeed, for those of us who accessed library collections, participated in study groups, and helped construct digital platforms during the Covid-19 lockdown, it is hard to imagine a strict distinction between e-studioing and studioing to ever return (in any strict sense).

Our claims will be as follows: The space-time opened up and sustained by the studio has been underappreciated as apart from the institutions and organizations of which it is a part. This means that the studio is paradoxically both inside and outside, public and private simultaneously. By providing a genealogy of the studio in Western history, we will highlight how the strange location of the studio foreshadows certain virtual dimensions of the postdigital sphere (that are not reducible to mere control and modulation). The unique educational logic that emerges from within the studio is study as the neutralization of the economy of learning. In this respect we stand with other theorists of study as an alternative to learning (Agamben 1995; Harney and Moten 2013; Lewis 2013; Ford 2016), but we make a stronger claim than many proponents of study and argue that study is a pataphysical educational logic. Drawing on the work of Alfred Jarry (1996), we see pataphysics as comprising the following key dimensions: it is a science that pursues (non)knowledge of exceptions and singularities (rather than metaphysical generalities), through a-disciplinary means, in order to discover/produce/create impossible solutions.[4] In educational language, pataphysics renders inoperative the metaphysics of learning, suspends the functioning of any learning-testing apparatus by neutralizing the means-end logic that ties education to larger forces of economization. While the "science of pataphysics attempts no cures, envisages no progress, distrusts all claims of 'improvement' in the state of things" (Shattuck 1960, 28), so too does a pataphysics of study necessarily insert a drift within university education away from that which it has become, pushing it out-of-bounds of itself by taking up and playing with its infrastructure in institutionally reckless though creative ways that defy calculation, planning, and quantification.

Finally, there is a unique kind of writing that accompanies the pataphysics of study within the space-time of the studio. We call this activity "protocol writing," which offers up simple yet often times paradoxical rules for impractical, ritualistic study. Whereas theorists have argued that the essential morphology of the university consists of the activity of lecturing within the space of the lecture hall (Marin 2020), we argue that this misses how universities also contain studio spaces that are apart from / a part of their infrastructure, enabling different kinds of writing that lend themselves to different kinds of study practices. Emerging from within the studio space as a formulation of study rules, protocols are not means to another end (as with lecture notes) but rather are means that open themselves up to circular forms of studious drift. These protocols may never make it to the lecture podium (in one form or another) because they are secret formulae for study that are often not com-

---

4. For more on pataphysics, see Hugill 2015 and Lewis 2020.

municable to others. Together, the space-time of the studio, the contemplation and experimentation of study, and the experimental writing of protocols form practices of *studioing*.

To formulate an educational theory of studioing, we will turn to an eclectic group of theorists, artists, and historians. In particular, we will use these reference points to envision a new kind of online educational experience beyond e-learning, one that takes up the very platforms and applications designed for learning and pirates them, rendering them inoperative in order to cultivate an experimental space whose outcomes cannot be determined in advance by the economic operationalism of the metaphysics of learning. Instead, we will offer an alternative, paradoxical space-time pataphysical machine of studioing that can be made common through postdigital piracy. Throughout we will make reference to Studio_D, mentioned above, which will act as a germinal resource for describing what education might look like and feel like in an online environment that challenges the metaphysics of learning while still preserving the potentiality of studenthood (as an educational life of study). It is our wager that this experiment can act as an exception to the metaphysical laws of learning (learnification), becoming a singularity or exception that can inspire other forms of study within the pataphysically blurry space-time of postdigital higher education.

And in the end, perhaps another university can become possible: a pataphysical university. Such universities can be absurdist, as with Walter Benjamin's playfully imaginative University of Muri in which all the buildings are made of chocolate and newly acquired library books include titles such as *Jewish Army Chaplain and Wood Imp* and (the classic) *The Easter Egg: Its Advantages and Dangers* (Benjamin 2012, 243). Or we can think of the College of Pataphysics with its absurd rituals, parodic reverence, and esoteric hierarchies (as well as its phynancial fees). Although extreme, both cases demonstrate an attempt to profane the university and its romantic if not sacred standing among public institutions. In addition to these tongue-and-cheek examples, there are now many calls for various spin-offs of the colonialist, anti-Black first-world university model, including the third-world university (la paperson 2017) and the abolition university (Meyerhoff, 2019) as well as parainstitutions such as Caitlin Cherry's Dark Study program. We stand in solidarity with these calls, but would also argue that the pataphysics of the university we will highlight in this book is not simply another addition to the list. Instead, a pataphysical dimension underlies and informs all these other variants insofar as they are *imaginary solutions*. Imaginary does not mean impossible. Indeed, flashes of such universities are immanent to the present moment. Imaginary in this case means that they take imagination to recognize, hold onto, use, and theorize. They take imagination to envision and experiment with (in often times fugitive, illicit, and/or reckless ways that fundamentally challenge probabilities and modulations). As such, the pataphysics of studioing and studying should be thought of not as supplements of existing calls for a reconstructed university but rather as the first step (or leap) into another educational dimension out of which an educational multiverse (one that is not defined solely by the metaphysics of learning) can become actuated.

1. The Studio: A Queer History

LOOKING AT THE HISTORY OF STUDIOS, the first observation is how pliable the space of the studio has been and is becoming. The scope of what constitutes a studio has been endlessly debated and reconfigured: sometimes a private, inward space of contemplation, seclusion, and creation and other times a public, outward space of collaboration. Think here of the seemingly insurmountable gap that separates the studio of Alberto Giacometti, which was once described by Alexander Liberman as a physical embodiment of the artist's private work process and his personal ego (Liberman 1960), and Andy Warhol's Factory, which manufactured art through collective processes overseen by the artist-as-celebrity rather than artist-as-genius. We might also juxtapose the living collage of Kurt Schwitters' studio or Fancis Bacon's studio as "compost heap" with the emptiness of Mark Rothko's sterile, puritanical studio (O'Doherty 2007). A similar list can be compiled for the scholar's studio. On the one hand, there is the quiet, orderly, and solitary studio of the Renaissance humanist who sits lost in thought, versus the rather chaotic, noisy, and cluttered studio of the alchemist as scholar juggling various experiments and familial relationships (Algazi 2012). And, at the furthest edge of recognizability, the term "studio" came to mean "drawing" during the early modern period, while during the twentieth century, it became associated with the artist's body itself. In short, the space of the studio seems to defy clear definition and boundaries.

In order to understand the pliability of the studio, we offer a brief (and necessarily incomplete) survey of verbal and visual depictions of studios from the Middle Ages up to the contemporary moment. This means we will run the gamut of what counts as a studio in order to draw out certain aspects of the idea of the studio that, we feel, are essential for understanding its pliability. In this sense, we see images of studios—from ancient to modern, from written to visually depicted/photographed—as the studio reflecting on its own possibility, its own potentiality. Agamben once wrote, "Lo studio è l'immagine della potenza—della potenza di scriverer per lo scrittore, della potenza di dipingere o scolpire per il pittore o lo scultore [The studio is the image of potentiality—of the potentiality to write for the writer, of the potentiality to paint or sculpt for the painter or the sculptor]" (2017, 13). In this sense, depictions of the studio throughout history are not an attempt to actualize the potentiality of the studio (in terms of specific outcomes whether they be scholarship, works of art, or other products) so much as to capture the moment when the potentiality for thinking thinks itself, or when the potentiality for painting paints itself. Using our terminology, such depictions attempt to make intelligible the open-ended pliability defining the potentiality to think, write, sculpt, or paint manifest across historical forms of studios.

From Studio to Studioing

The history of the studio/study is composed of social, cultural, and economic drift, revealing its essential pliability. The studio (also referred to as the *studiolo, museum,* or *studorium*) spread from high-ranking scholars of the Middle Ages, to Renaissance artists, to teachers and country pastors, ultimately becoming a rather common feature of middle-class households. In other words, over time, strict dichotomies between the wealth of courtly studios and those of the lower classes began to erode. In addition, courtly and aristocratic studios, such as Leonello d'Este's, were not always private affairs, but were opened up for visitation by scholars of various ranks and also artists who in turn popularized the notion of the studio to a wider public (Thornton 1998). As recorded in the writings of Benedetto Varchi, the act of drawing came to resemble the act of thinking (*designo* could equally mean the drawing and form of an idea), and artists and scholars began to look similar and occupy similar studio spaces despite potentially different social backgrounds—cramped with books, drawings, scientific devices, and various classical statues/models (Cole and Pardo 2005). In addition to crossing boundaries between craft and contemplation, by the late sixteenth century in Europe, the studio was no longer an "extraordinary privilege" of the rich and influential but had also become part of scholars' and artists' homes, "even humble ones" (Algazi 2012, 18). In other words, the diffusion of the medieval *studium* (which applied equally to a monk's cell or the library of a religious house) to secular *estudes* of fourteenth-century courtly aristocracy in France, to the *studioli* of fifteenth- and sixteenth-century Italian scholars, demonstrated the pliability of the idea of the studio.

Pliability in this context has three meanings: first, in terms of use; second, in terms of actual, physical space (extension in relation to size and shape); and third, in terms of location. Despite such variety and heterogeneity, we want to hazard some generalizations that will enable us to pinpoint how it is that the potentiality of the studio preserves itself across diverse manifestations. Instead of erasing the plasticity of the studio space by providing a rather reductive definition, we want to generate criteria that can take into account the pliability we have been describing. What is it about the studio that makes it so pliable in the first place? What are the *minimum* conditions that enable studios to be called studios while also keeping open the seemingly indeterminate potentialities of studios for reconfiguring themselves? Our assumption in posing this questions is simple: that there are sufficient commonalities across studios that make the term intelligible as an open-ended idea. If collections such as *The Studio Reader* or *The Studio* chart the rhizomatic diffusion of the studio, then we want to gather together the various strands and organize them around three dimensions. These dimensions can then serve as the basic or minimal criteria for defining the specific pliability/potentiality of the studio.

First, while clear distinctions are fuzzy, a studio is a space separate from a workshop, a gallery, a classroom, and the more overtly "functional" parts of the home (like the kitchen). It is not a place where apprentices are taught or where art is displayed for public viewing or where the household is managed by the paterfamilias. Studios, in this sense, are a way of partitioning off a space from certain obligations that are oriented toward instruction, commerce, and management. They are spaces wherein expertise (of the teacher), value (of the merchant), and authority (of the household manager) are in some sense *deactivated* or *rendered inoperative*. Two early examples of this can be found in the studio spaces of Tintoretto and Michelangelo (Cole and Pardo 2005). In both cases, the studio was reserved for working on designs and prototypes and was a privileged space for contemplative activities as distinct from the artistic labors of the workshop where assistants were taught and major commissions carried out.

Sadly, the majority of depictions of early studios show them as isolated spaces dominated largely by men and guarded by a dog from intrusion by women and children. The privacy and solitude that the studio seems to offer is, therefore, the privilege of men at the expense of women and children who must be shut out. In reflecting on Edmund Husserl's writing desk, Sara Ahmed points out the gendered dimension of his studio space. Extrapolating from Husserl's description of his writing desk, Ahmed writes, "The study, the room dedicated to writing or other forms of contemplation, conjures up such a vivid image of a masculine domain at the front of the house" (2006, 30). At stake in Ahmed's phenomenology of Husserl's phenomenology of his writing desk is how such spaces are formed against an invisible backdrop of other household spaces occupied by women and children that are erased through Husserl's phenomenological reduction of the desk. In this way, the desk becomes the property of certain male bodies at the exclusion of women, who are relegated to other rooms of the house (such as the kitchen). The studio and its equipment, including the writing desk, are oriented toward certain male bodies that are called to take up writing and contemplating.

Certainly Ahmed's description is a persuasive one, pointing toward the gendered history of the studio. Taking up Ahmed's theoretical position, we would like to further *queer* the notion of the studio in two senses. First, we want to highlight the marginal or minor tradition of female scholars at work in the studio, as witnessed in the depiction of Christine de Pizan sitting at her desk accompanied with her dog from 1407 (Cole and Padro 2005). Stated simply, there is nothing intrinsic about the studio that binds it necessarily to male bodies.[1] Second, while it is historically accurate to emphasize connections between male privilege and the studio, we would like to offer a counter reading in which the studio is a space that interrupts the management of the household by the male sovereign, suspending his authority to rule over others. Granted, the studio was (and is) defined by a certain amount of seclusion from the shared family quarters (thus securing the silence needed for contemplation, even if such security could never be guaranteed), perhaps we could also read the presence of the dog in many depictions of the studio not as guarding the male studier from others (unwanted intruders) so much as guarding others from the powers of the paterfamilias, now rendered inoperative in and through the act of contemplation.

At stake in the idea of the studio is that it deactivates relationships marked by authority (of teacher over student or husband over wife) and commerce (as the exchange of goods for money) in the name of contemplation and experimentation. The theme of deactivation permeates images of studio spaces and is, in some ways, epitomized in the figure of the sleeping dog at the foot of the scholar or artist. As Algazi argues, the dog articulates a specific form of scholarly solitude: "not simply the wish to be alone, to avoid others' company, but to have company at will without entangling oneself in a

---

1. See also the essays collected in Selmi 2008.

web of reciprocal obligations" (2012, 32). The dog and scholar are intimate yet somewhat indifferent to one another. In other words, the relationship between the scholar and the dog can be read paradoxically as a relational nonrelation or a relation of being together by being mutually indifferent to one another, or mutually indifferent to *obligations* defining specific, functional roles between teachers and students, husbands and wives, artists and patrons. Without exaggerating this point too much, the implication here seems to be that the studio offers a *free* space where a *noninstrumental* contact between self and other becomes possible, liberated from economic relations of management, instruction, or commerce.

Another important dimension of the studio is that it was originally conceptualized as a space of radical innovation and experimentation that was a-disciplinary in spirit (indeed, they preexisted the disciplinary demarcations that define the current state of affairs in the academy). The artist-as-student was positioned somewhere between craftsman and scholar, and the studio as the artist's space also implied a space of study and scientific research. Leonardo da Vinci's studio is paradigmatic in this sense. It is where he experimented with new pigments, with dissection, and with various scientific and alchemical principles. His notebooks *as* studios could be read as equal parts research manuscript and artistic expression. In sum, the studio was, as Michael Cole and Mary Pardo summarize (2005), a kind of microcosm that could just as easily be a place of contemplation as a place of painting, an anatomy theater, a laboratory, a kitchen, and a monastic cell. For a more contemporary example of this a-disciplinarity, we can turn to Marcel Duchamp and a famous description of his studio. Herbert Molderings highlights how Duchamp used the studio to experiment with epistemic objects (such as readymades) that did not function to illustrate existing knowledge but rather to exemplify devices that generate "unknown answers to questions that the scientist still cannot formulate clearly" (2007, 150). The studio for Duchamp was therefore a place neither of art nor science but rather an experimental zone that existed in the gap that separates and combines the two distinct disciplines.

The readymades objectified a new kind of nonknowledge that could not be easily subsumed within the calculative reasoning of science or the aesthetic canons of art. The studio, as Molderings aptly states, was a "laboratory of experimental perception and theory" (151).

And finally, in the early Renaissance, studios were not retreats from the outside world. Although it is common to think of the studio as hermetically sealed and secured against outside intrusion, this is not necessarily the case. Indeed, studios offered unique contact points between inside and outside. By 1600, the *studiolo* was also referred to as a museum and was associated with collecting. As Cole and Pardo (2005) point out, the studio became a "sort of microcosm" that could contain any number of books (on a wide range of topics, ancient and modern, scientific and religious), instruments (globes, clocks, pens, inkwells, and armillary spheres), and artifacts (signet rings, mirrors, cabinets of wonder, and exotic items from around the world), each gesturing beyond themselves toward a world that was present in its absence. Indeed, we would argue that the studio is not a retreat from the world but rather a *suspension* of the world so that it can be studied. Thus, the world exists as a virtual idea in the studio, and this ensures that the studio is always already oriented beyond itself.[2]

The contamination of the hermeticism of the studio continues as a theme and practice throughout the centuries. For instance, artist's studios in the twentieth century were not sealed, sterilized envelopes reflecting the genius of the artist back to him or herself

2. While it is important to point out that the collections that filled studio spaces were, at least in part, the result of colonialism (and an attending desire to order and classify the world), it is also important to note how the marvelous assortment of natural objects, human artifacts, magical implements, and scientific instruments found in studios present fluid and ambiguous meanings that undermine any attempt to characterize them neatly in terms of "meta-realities" such as colonialism, oppression, or possession (Kemp 1995). These collections refused to submit to precise categorization (as status symbol, for instance), and thus embody a distinctly pataphysical potential for igniting curiosities that betray colonialist agendas.

so much as permeable membranes shot through with the objects of the world. Thus, as O'Doherty points out, many studios were littered with various magazines, books, and odd bits and pieces of culture, all of which referenced the outside world while at the same time suspending the immediacy and necessity of this outside world. Indeed, the main question artists such as Fancis Bacon asked, according to O'Doherty (2007, 21), was: "Could it be used?" Just as the scholar suspended the world in order to study it, so too the artist brought the outside into the studio, freeing up the outside for new use beyond everyday functionality.

Although the studio can be read as a spatial inscription of a withdrawal from the world and the rise in a new, modern sense of the private individual (Webb 2007), it might also be interpreted as the *impossibility* of such a construction, as the individual is always already contaminated by the outside. Dora Thornton (1998) makes a similar point in that the studio has always been oriented around a broader public—conveying a certain amount of worldly esteem upon the owner—even if it was oriented toward a private, internal world of thought and creation. Thus the studio was, in some ways, a paradoxical space wherein the very mark of privacy, solitude, and inwardness was itself a *public* performance dependent on those who were absent from the studio. Sometimes such solitude was literally and intentionally broken as with the "convivial study" (Thornton 1998, 120), which was a space to be shared with and visited by scholars, artists, orators, collectors, and poets, but even if this was not the case, the "isolation" of the studio was, in some way, gesturing beyond itself toward a virtual community.

Here we find a complex relationship between inside and outside, self and other inscribed in the paradoxical space of the studio. Inspired by Kafka's work, Deleuze and Guattari describe a solitary "artistic singularity" as someone who desires "both to be alone and to be connected to all the machines of desire. A machine that is all the more social and collective insofar as it solitary . . . [by] tracing the line of escape, [it] is equivalent in itself to a community whose conditions haven't yet been established" (1986, 71). The artistic singularity and the virtual community form two sides of a collective assemblage, even if the "objective conditions of this community are not yet given." (84). In their book *Dialogues,* Deleuze and Claire Parnet return to this idea and link it directly to the studio. They write, "When Godard says he would like to be a production studio, he is obviously not trying to say that he wants to produce his own films, or he wants to edit his own books. He is trying to say just ideas, because, when it comes down to it, you are all alone, and yet you are like a conspiracy of criminals. You are no longer an author, you are a production studio, you have never been more populated" (Deleuze and Parnet 1996, 15–16). One becomes the studio—a collective assemblage that is both parts internal and external, singular and plural. This assemblage is criminal in that it only appears on stolen time, or rather time *freed* from official business (in the middle of the night, when one cannot sleep . . .). In sum, the studio is a space for connecting up multiple desiring machines that turn inward and outward; circle around private practices of self-cultivation and public performances of one's knowledge, creativity, and ingenuity; interrupt one's responsibilities and official duties in order to constitute a new kind of virtual and criminal community lived through the potentiality for contemplation that is cradled by the studio. There is always a virtual community present even if that community is unnamed and unknown (or to come).

Additionally, it is important to remember that one of the first conceptual models for the early modern scholar's studio was the hermit's wilderness retreat. For instance, in the last years of the fourteenth century, the Florentine notary Ser Lapo Mazzei described his experience of sitting in his *studio* as "the happiness of the good hermits on the mountain" (cited in Webb 2007, 167). In the hermit's experiment with solitary, mountain dwelling, the scholar found a model for the "cultivation of perplexity, or losing one's way in order to find one's way" (Wood 2005, 62). This quest for "voluntary bewilderment" (62) is, as Christopher Wood argues, the origin of the modern studio. And the studio never lost this connection with the idea of the wilderness. Indeed, as artists began to turn increasingly toward natural sciences and observation, they traveled outside, transforming nature itself into a studio.

Another example of the porous relationship between inside and outside that defines the space of the studio is found in the history of the camera obscura. Astronomers in the sixteenth century used pinholes in darkened studios to study solar phenomena (Renner 2004). The studio—even as a black box—was never sealed from the outside. Rather, the inside became a projection screen or a technology for observing the outside. Thus there is a push and pull between inside and outside, inwardness and outwardness, singularity and plurality that is at the crux of the studio. If Wood argues that the studio is a kind of "nonplace" that is in constant dialogue with the pasture, the medieval workshop, and the modern university, then such a nonplace is less utopia than a-topia, or a place that is a-part of other places (both inside and outside). As Agamben might argue, it is a special limbo wherein ideas are neither saved nor damned but rather blissfully left "without destination" (1993, 6). Again, easy dichotomies between inside and outside, privacy and publicity, nature and culture that the studio seems to reinforce are actually rendered inoperative by the studio.

Many of these traits are exemplified in depictions of the decisively queer studios of those "bad scholars" known as alchemists. Depictions of the alchemist's studio contradict the more or less secluded study of the (male) scholar. Instead, the studio is bursting with energy and activity. Experiments are undertaken by male alchemists and their wives, thus undercutting the gendered division of labor often found in images of scholarly studios. Children, apprentices, servants, and others mix and mingle in relation to a shared activity of experiment. If these images, as Algazi argues (2012), were read at the time as illustrating what *not* to do as a scholar, our point is somewhat different: studios are spaces wherein scholars can and do go astray, places in which categories, roles, and divisions of labor are mixed, and where hierarchies and dichotomies (such as inside and outside) can be rendered inoperative. Rather than merely the antithesis of the well-ordered, secluded space of the scholar, we see the alchemist studio as exemplifying latent tendencies within the studio itself. Think here of Duchamp's studio as a more contemporary variant of the alchemist's workspace. The various activities that defined and still define such studios— everything from observation, experimentation, illicit exploration, and contemplation—convey the pliability of the studio as a para- doxical space of queer transgressions (sometimes despite itself).

Although studios were part of the compartmentalization of space during the early modern period (especially in relation to the household), these were also boundary-crossing spaces. In sum the studio is (a) a place wherein power can be deactivated (beyond the economic management of households or classrooms), (b) an a- disciplinary zone of experimentation, and (c) a paradoxical location (un)bounded by divisions of public/private, inside/outside (they both inaugurate such divisions while simultaneously embodying their impossibility or permeability).

Finally, there is the time of the studio. In his book titled *Autoritratto nello Studio* (2017), Agamben touches upon the unusual temporality of the studio. Dwelling in the studio offers a unique- ly paradoxical sensation of time captured in the phrase "festina lente" (69) or making haste slowly. This is the time of contemplation opened up by and through the inoperativity and a-disciplinarity of the studio. When in the studio, one is lost in the ritual of study (see chapter 2) in which one feels equal parts progressing and digressing, patience and anticipation/eagerness. Time seems to both stop and accelerate when in the studio. O'Doherty (2007) also gives a par- adoxical formulation to studio time as a "mobile cluster of tenses, quotas of past embodied in completed works, some abandoned, others waiting for resurrection, at least one in process occupying a nervous present, through which, as James Joyce said, future plunges into past, a future exerting on the present the pressure of unborn ideas" (18). This is not a linear time of productivity in which proj- ects are undertaken for commission and work progresses toward a final end. Instead, the temporality of the studio is nonlinear, queer, a multiplicity of tenses all intersecting with one another. The works all seem to be suspended—some abandoned, others waiting for resurrection, and others occupying a "nervous present" in which their completion does not seem certain (or even desired). In this sense, the studio is a peculiar kind of time machine that de-completes what is completed, and completes what is de-completed in various tenses that do not seem to exist. O'Doherty summarizes: "Time is reversed, revised, discarded, used up" (18). In this sense, the work of the studio is really work on and with time as its medium. Backward and forward, before and after, earlier and later can no longer be strictly separated and divided, leading to paradoxical phenomenologies of slow haste and progression through digression. Stated differently, the time of the studio is as pliable as its spatial dimensions. And if this is the case, it is incorrect to think of the studio simply as a space (a container) of actions. Instead, we ought to think of the studio as a process: the process of studioing.

It is the idea of the studio as studioing that we wish to rehabilitate in this book. The result is not an attempt to *return to* the studio as it has been historically configured. Instead, it is to redeem those features of studioing that maximize its pliability. In this sense, we agree with some aspects of the poststudio movement in the arts that argue that the studio is too restrictive and exclusive (often attached to a romantic notion of the solitary, male genius), opting instead for thinking about art-making as a collaborative, social practice, dispersed throughout communities while also complicating any strict separation between production and distribution (Caroline Jones 1996; Caitlin Jones 2010). These are valid points that we want to hold onto. High modernism, in particular, transformed the studio into an object, a fetish, that ends with the celebrity artist in *his* celebrity studio. As O'Doherty warns (2007), this reification of the studio—as a product for art world consumption—is a domestication of the studio as a radical process. At the same time, we find the essential aspects of studioing—as an experimental zone that prefers not to abide by the rules defining classroom norms, household management, or market economization—still having potentiality for new uses.

From Studioing to Pataphysical Time
Machine and Back Again

The studio as a *space* adjacent (to instruction, management, and commerce) is also a *pace* adjacent (to the time of production, which is more or less linear and governed by deadlines, outputs, and contracts/obligations). The s-pace of the studio is therefore a-part of the household, university, or workshop, meaning that it is a part that has no part, containing within it time that might be lost and activities that might not be productive. It is a space-time in which the scholar–artist loses him or herself in contemplation or experimentation that does not have an end or perhaps does not even desire one. As adjacent, the studio opens up to and makes manifest a *pataphysical dimension* with various institutions (such as the household). To studio is to experiment with virtual space-times that are neither here nor there, inside nor outside, past nor future. This pataphysical dimension of the studio has already been consciously explored by artists themselves. Take for instance Edward Krasinski's studio, which he turned into a pataphysical experiment full of alchemical magic capable of suspending the laws of physics all the while embracing impossible solutions (Mytkowska and Pryzywara 2004). To conclude this chapter, we will expand on the theoretical possibilities opened up by Krasinski and others, reframing the idea of the studio as a kind of pataphysical space-time machine and studioing as a practice of tinkering with temporality.

On the one hand, we agree with Phillip Zarrilli when he writes that the studio is a space and time defined by a "fundamental paradox" (2002, 159). For Zarrilli, this paradox can be broken down into various questions that, in one way or another, ensure that the studioing remains a practice without ends or goals. The studio, on this reading, is a perpetual premise or question rather than a declaration or decision. Stated differently, the studio, according to Zarrilli, is a pure means (without end) rather than a means directed toward an end, or even an end in itself. Concurring with Zarrilli, we have been highlighting the pliability of the studio as an open potentiality—as manifest in images and descriptions of various studios throughout history, each of which becomes a meditation on the ability to think or to create. At the same time, we reject Zarrilli's insistence that the studio be defined in terms of a specific metaphysics that would connect it to an eternal Law that is transcendental, necessary, and universal. Instead, we want to develop the thesis that the essential paradox that Zarrilli highlights is not metaphysical so much as pataphysical, meaning that it emerges from a suspension of metaphysical Law in order to reveal new possible modes of thinking, acting, creating, and being from that which remains in limbo (and in this sense is anarchic).

It is worthwhile noting that pataphysics was established in an a-disciplinary fashion, first appearing in Alfred Jarry's Ubu plays. The origin in theater is not accidental or inconsequential but rather situates pataphysics as a radical practice unconcerned with the norms or standards of hard science, or even those of art itself. Still, this is not so much a repudiation of science as it is a demonstration of how pataphysics exists beyond any particular method or genre. Pataphysical dimensions are opened up concurrently with those of "reality" and "common sense," allowing for unexpected resonances across disciplines and experience. The pataphysical dimension is in a sense overlaid onto the everyday world, revealing latent potentialities. Jarry's book *Exploits & Opinions of Dr. Faustroll, Pataphysician* both seeks to define and enact pataphysics through an unconventional form that is novelistic, pseudoscientific, taxonomic, philosophical, bureaucratic, dialogic, and epistolary by turns. It begins with a visit to the good doctor by the bailiff, Panmuphle, who is delivering an official notice of warrant. But the bailiff quickly has to abandon his official duties and leave behind his stamped papers so as to go on a fantastical journey with Dr. Faustroll. What appears to be a bed actually turns out to be a peculiar space-time machine that Dr. Faustroll describes as a floating skiff that can travel to distant lands (and perhaps alternative time periods) without actually leaving Paris. Thus, the pataphysical space of the skiff as space-time machine renders inoperative divisions between inside and outside, here and there, private (a personal bed) and public (a collective skiff).

Accompanying Dr. Faustroll and Panmuphle are, as the doctor explains, "some beings who have managed to escape your Law and your Justice between the lines of my seized volumes" (1996, 17). The skiff is in exodus from official Law, both in terms of state law and laws of physics, opening up a "universe supplementary to this one" (21). In this sense, there is something that is equal parts imaginative and fugitive about the experimentation with space and time that Dr. Faustroll undertakes. It does not reside within the coordinates of any known system of measurement, and does not obey any known law of humanity or nature. Thus it is fitting that the journey begins with the abduction of a bailiff, who in turn gives up trying to record the strange events that unfold as "retained for the Law and Justice" (14).

The investigation undertaken by the travelers follows the tenants of an unnamed science of pataphysics that challenges existing rules and regulations regarding what counts as knowledge. Neither inductive nor deductive, pataphysical investigations search for singularities. As Dr. Faustroll states, it is the "science of the particular" (21). Since science concerns the search for laws, not only does pataphysics interrupt existing Law and Justice but also the search for Law and Justice as appropriate ends. Instead, what emerges is an engagement with particulars as particulars (or peculiarities) that can only be examples of themselves (without comparison or measure). In emphasizing the particular, the goal is not so much to generate synthesis across particulars so much as to produce alchemical relationships between particulars to see what emerges, even if the chain reaction might, as Deleuze warns (1995a), explode the faculties. In this sense, pataphysics fully embodies an a-disciplinary and feral approach to experimenting with the boundaries defining what is real.

To suspend Law and Justice means that restraints and ordering principles and practices are left idle so that ideas and techniques can suddenly be opened up for new uses. For Dr. Faustroll, science, math, symbolism, and occult practices all collide in the form of pataphysical experimentation on the fringes of reality. The time that opens up within such spaces is one that is discontinuous, interrupting divisions constituting or structuring a certain, linear flow of events from beginning to end, from potentiality to actualization, from past to present to future. Experientially, one is caught in a slow haste, or a rhythmic drifting back and forth, where progress and regress are never clearly defined or delineated. As such, there is no clear exit from the pataphysical experiment once it ensues. This is a time of suspension, when clocks cease to function, and where time as an arrow bends back on itself.

While more can be said about pataphysical exploration of a supplementary world in exodus from Law and Justice, what we want to emphasize here is the connection between the pataphysical space-time machine of the bed-as-skiff and studioing. Considering the frequency with which studios were located in or adjacent to bed-chambers in the early modern period, it is perhaps not surprising that Jarry takes up his bed as the locus for a pataphysical (if not alchemical) experimentation in studioing. Furthermore, just as modern artists such as Phyllida Barlow, Graham Sussin, Simon Starling, Keith Tyson, and Keith Wilson describe their studio practice as a kind of journey or travel (Wood 2005), so too does Jarry's pataphysics produce its own kind of journey that plays with the very parameters of inside and outside, production and display, private and public, distance and nearness, past and future. Through pataphysical appropriation and experimentation, Dr. Faustroll's bed is freed from its function as a private space and time for sleep and unleashed for new, collective uses by his motley crew. It is, in other words, a pataphysical epistemic object for producing (queer) nonknowledge. Likewise, studios have a similar potential: taking up objects from the outside world and rendering them inoperative in order to experiment with perceptual and epistemic possibilities. In both cases, we are presented with paradoxical locations outside familiar coordinates of inside and outside, public and private. Temporally, both offer a confluence of tenses that projects the past and the future into the present. And finally, we find the deactivation of divisions of labor and subject positions as an underlying continuity between Jarry's pataphysical experiments and the history of the studio. The bailiff finds the Law inadequate, the doctor is a doctor of a science that has no name and is "illegitimate," and the traveling companion, Bosse-de-Nage, is a talking baboon that thinks he is human. This motley crew of mis-fits does not seem to have a destination or a destiny. Instead, they are adrift in the pataphysical universe of singular islands, each stranger than its predecessor, riding on a skiff that is mobile in its immobility.

Early on in the book, Faustroll explains that the "skiff is not only propelled by oar blades but also by suction disks at the end of spring levers. And its keel travels on three steel rollers at the same level" (Jarry 1996, 17). A sieve of intricate meshes that can progress on land or water, the skiff would be at home in an alchemist's studio, or that of Duchamp. One could also imagine a drawing of such a vessel among Da Vinci's renderings of inventions, machinery, and military equipment. Elsewhere, Faustroll offers another definition of pataphysics as "the science of imaginary solutions" (22). The skiff presents itself as a remedy for Faustroll's legal troubles, navigating a pataphysical dimension that has been superimposed onto his daily life. The absurd utility of the vessel stems from its status as "imaginary solution." Within pataphysics, the problems themselves can be real or imagined, but the solutions are always situated in a zone where such divisions are meaningless. Studioing occurs within this zone a-part from all others.

Although Jarry focuses on Dr. Faustroll's bed as a pataphysical space-time machine, we would also like to highlight how Dr. Faustroll's library seems to be designed to throw into high relief the pataphysical potentials latent in the collections of books, objects, and devices that characterize the clutter of studios. Close to the beginning of Jarry's *Faustroll*, the character Panmuphle lists the books contained in the pataphysician's library. As Ben Fisher has argued, this catalogue is a rather "perverse selection" characterised by a "deliberately idiosyncratic quality" (2001, 26–27). While

Fisher argues that the catalogue can be interpreted as evidence of the eclecticism of the Symbolist style in general, he is also careful to emphasise the irreducible singularity of Jarry's manner of organising the library (thus interrupting any attempt to form generalizations out of particulars). Of course, Jarry's list is presented in alphabetical order, but this convention only manages to throw into relief how such order is artificial if not absurdist, ultimately suspending its own appearance of "order." Instead, the books (high and low literature, religious and scientific, historical and fictional) set up the conditions for odd encounters and a-disciplinary forms of nonknowledge. Just as studioing queers objects (suspending destinations and functions), so too does Jarry's library queer the books that it contains, disorienting them through strange juxtapositions and unauthorized intimacies. In short, the pataphysician's studio—composed of odd devices (the skiff), books, and experimentations with time and space—is not a studio but *the* paradigm of studioing, meaning that it makes studioing as a process intelligible precisely because of its extreme deviance.

But we can press this thesis even further. The river upon which Dr. Faustroll's skiff drifts is not a river of water so much as a river of "ethernity" (Jarry 1996, 104), which is "circularly mobile and perishable," a "luminiferous ether," an "elastic solid" (104). Ethernity is not fixed and immobile (like eternity), but nor is it simply a chemical ether with physical properties that can be identified and measured by science. Instead, it is a pataphysical substance that exists before the very coordinates of space and time are divided up and calculated out. Studioing (as an experimental, a-disciplinary, a-topic, and paradoxical suspension that is a-part from that which it is a part) emerges out of ethernity, and ethernity is made manifest in and through studioing. In this sense, the pliability of the studio that we have emphasized in this chapter is a material manifestation of ethernity as an elastic solid, as a spatial and temporal process of emergence that bucks up against the homogenous, organized space and time defined by any metaphysical Law.

The virtual sphere of ethernity will, in our project, connect the studio to the equally elastic and circularly mobile virtual sphere of postdigital space and time. At this point, we can return to a problem that Caroline A. Jones once posited to artists concerning the relationship between their studio practice and emergent social, technological, and artistic transformations brought about by advanced digital and information systems. At the end of her book *Machine in the Studio: Constructing the Postwar American Artist,* she provocatively speculates: "Chances are, artists won't be drawn back to the studio—but if they are, it will be a radically different place than it was in 1948. Machines are now so deep in our imaginary that we are cultural, if not yet biological, cyborgs; we are soft-wired for technology in our desiring machines" (1996, 373). Through technological advancements, studioing has become increasingly socialized and expanded beyond the traditional notions of the studio, thus putting the very concept at risk of being eclipsed by poststudio practices. Yet our wager is that emergent postdigital spaces maximize the essential pliability of studioing, disseminating it and stretching it even further than artists and scholars have henceforth imagined. The internet, in particular, is a *technology* of ethernity that makes studioing a new possibility for a wide array of participants. Simply put, postdigital interplay between digital, biological, cultural, and artifactual dimensions of experience need not be seen as erasing the studio but rather extending and intensifying the potentiality of studioing. In the next chapter we will explore the implications of this for postpandemic e-learning in the university.

2. Studying Online: Virtual Studio Spaces

THUS FAR we have outlined the pataphysical space-time machine of the studio. We have done so by returning to images of the studio that might indeed seem rather ancient or antiquated. But what do these images have to tell us now, in this moment of e-learning? This is a pressing problem. It would seem that while digital interfaces hold some promise for expanding and intensifying the pataphysics of the studio, digital platforms are also consistently constrained by institutional limitations placed upon them—for example, as through Learning Management Systems (LMS). The question facing educators in an era of increasing e-learning concerns the type of space and time of education as it exists in the gap that separates and conjoins the virtual and the actual, the material and the immaterial. Will the rise of pandemic e-learning interfaces become yet another form of control, or can postdigital experimental zones be envisioned as pataphysical studio space-time situations?

These questions are educational equivalents to those first asked by Johanna Drucker in her reflections on the rise of digital humanities in the university. On the one hand, digital tools and platforms have offered new and exciting research opportunities for humanistic inquiry. On the other hand, insights into complexities of interpretation have often been subordinated to the practical requirements and constraints of computational protocols. In other words, the digital humanities have historically maintained the primacy and authority of computational methods inscribed within logical systems. The result was, according to Drucker, the forced concession of many insights gained through critical, social, and deconstructionist theory to the functionality of workable, transparent, accurate, efficient, and solution-oriented standards of data access and display. In sum, Drucker warns, "Theoretical issues that arise are, therefore, intimately bound to practical tasks, and all the lessons of deconstruction and poststructuralism—the extensive critiques of reason and grand narratives, the recognition that presumptions of objectivity are merely cultural assertions of particular, historical formations—threaten to disappear under the normalizing pressures of digital protocols" (2009, 7). Drucker's formulation of speculative computing attempted to render inoperative the instrumental and standardized approach to digital humanities through experiments at SpecLab. It also did so by returning to the infrastructure of knowledge production and distribution, hacking into its ordered and rational systems to produce complexity, ambiguity, and a sense of imaginative play. These "aesthetic provocations" (18) were directly informed by Jarry's pataphysics. No longer conceptualized as a mechanistic tool for solving problems, computational protocols were reconceptualized as toys to be played with a la pataphysical "rules" for producing impossible solutions that posed their own problems. Speculative computing "is driven by a commitment to interpretation-as-deformance in a tradition that has its roots in parody, play, and critical methods such as those of the Situationist International, Oulipo, and the longer tradition of pataphysics with its emphasis on 'the particular' over 'the general'" (25).

For us, speculative computing is a kind of postdigital experimentation with technological and institutional infrastructure that releases pataphysical potentialities within systems otherwise defined by their mechanical functionality. The lessons Drucker offers from her experiments at SpecLab are instructive for educators now facing the challenge of teaching in hybrid or virtual formats. Indeed, the educational translation of Drucker's problematic concerns the ways in which the metaphysics of learning become inscribed within the very technological infrastructures that teachers and professors are required to employ in order to generate digital "classrooms." In this chapter, we will turn once again to Studio_D as an experiment undertaken at the very beginning of the pandemic in the United States that is poised between virtual and actual, material and immaterial dimensions of educational life.

Studio_D: Drifting toward Study

The spring semester of 2020 was truly unprecedented as college professors around the world had to suddenly pivot to online instruction as a response to the novel coronavirus pandemic. While there had been trends toward online learning systems in higher education for years, it seems likely that the accelerated changes provoked by coronavirus are here to stay. As such, this is an apt time to reflect on the learning metaphysics underlying the development of digital platforms now and in the foreseeable future. As Siân Bayne and colleagues point out (2020), digital education all too easily becomes a symptom of learnification discourses and attending notions of education as transactional and quantitative. Bayne's call for a new kind of speculative (dare we say pataphysical) approach to online teaching breaks with instrumental logics and welcomes "uncertainty, risk, complexity" (23). Furthering this line of inquiry, we offer up Studio_D as a platform for experimenting with the space and time of another kind of educational life: study.

But before we offer Studio_D as an example of e-study, we first want to sharpen the distinction between learning and studying first raised in our introduction, this time in relation to the phenomenological question of movement. We do so to make clear how the educational pataphysics of studioing concerns the unleashing and exploration of studious movements. Such a distinction might at first appear rather odd, considering that most illustrations of classrooms or studios depict individuals as sitting still. Yet despite such appearances, there is much movement in these spaces—movement that involves thinking as well as various gestures of learning and studying (such as writing, taking notes, reading, gazing, and so forth).

For instance, the gestures of learning might be referred to as gestures of work and communication. Drawing on Vilém Flusser (2014), such gestures are first and foremost directed at materials, and these materials are meant to communicate something to someone. The work of learning is to exhibit development, growth, or progress through the work one accomplishes (homework), and this work is meant to communicate to others what has been achieved. Learning as a gesture of work and communication is like the arrow of education, pointing to a future anterior state wherein ignorance will have been overcome by knowledge and deficits will have been overcome by mastery that, in turn, can be exhibited through works for others to inspect, grade, and evaluate. The learner has a certain intentional aim (such as learning how to play a sport), this intention helps organize a set of experiences, which can be evaluated according to certain success conditions (such as winning an increasing number of matches that convey mastery to peers, teachers, and fans). Throughout the development process, the intention is actualized through the apparent active force of the will, creating various manifestations of the potentiality to grow, develop, and progress toward an intended goal. When the going gets tough, the will steps in to help overcome moments in learning when the initial intention is not enough to sustain progress toward reaching success. The will, in other words, unites means to ends, suturing up the relationship through the concretization of works that externalize the learning process for the benefit of others to recognize according to a certain standard. Or perhaps more accurately, the will acts as a conceptual cover for nonintentional (unwilled) forces deeply harnessed to modes of production. In either case, the appearance of the will and its agency serves a key function within the narrative of learning, which focuses on producing works and communicating to others. This investment in the will exhibits a certain metaphysical commitment to controlling, predicting, and ultimately regulating/managing contingencies in the name of efficiency, excellence, and so on. Stated differently, one is tested so that educational systems can *predict* future outputs and to *manage* the direction of the educational arrow that is learning (even if the predictions are inaccurate). This is thus a game of probabilities, which determine what potentialities can and should be invested in, what kinds of debts should be taken on, and what kinds of returns can be expected. An entire economy builds around the arrow of learning in order to maintain the need for lifelong learning and testing.

As work and communication, learning is a movement that we might describe as *summiting*. At first, the aim is distant, and seems insurmountable. But through consistent, willful experiences, the aim can be approximated one step at a time. Fatigue might set in as the learner continues the arduous summiting process, but the will simultaneously develops its own fortitude and resiliency. A growing sense of progress is also, of course, encouraging to the learner who, from the vista of the summit, can gaze back over the long trail and take a certain amount of pride in the work completed. While various routes and paths might be available, the key point here is that they are predicated on the promise of summitting that enables the learner to stand above the various routes and paths and evaluate performance in order to communicate such performance to others. Or, even if such a cumulative moment never comes, the summit is still posited as a horizon that orients all pseudosummits and gives them meaning (as minor successes within a lifelong trajectory).

This type of educational movement can be contrasted to *browsing* the internet. Browsing lacks both (a) an overtly intentional directionality and (b) the appearance of willful struggle that is involved in learning-as-summiting. There is something casual and incidental about browsing that lacks intentional directedness. Likewise, there is little resistance online that might force one to exert willful force. Internet features such as *hyperlinking* help illustrate this point. Starting from any given webpage, it is entirely possible for one to click on hyperlinks indefinitely. Coming across a dead or broken link disrupts and underscores the perpetuating nature of browsing. Search engines also provide seemingly endless routes for exploration. Ironically, this "openness" of browsing more often than not ends up steering casual browsers into increasingly more and more tailored searches, resulting in a perpetual echo chamber in which there is never any exposure to otherness. Browsing, in this sense, becomes solipsistic—an illusion of "effortless" and "free" wandering that nevertheless increasingly restricts what can be seen and heard.[1] And finally, there are minimal success conditions to browsing. Because of this, there is no way for the learner to measure progress or regress. There is no summit to reach, no end that can definitively justify the means taken, no work that can be completed. Instead, there is a sense of skimming along a flat surface that lacks peaks and valleys. There is no topography here (no above or below). Instead, there is only a passive sense of undergoing (rather than willful undertaking). Hence the pervasive feeling of getting lost in the stream of content the internet offers.

The distinction between summitting and browsing is important to note as it sets up the problematic underlying e-learning. The struggle of e-learning is how to ensure the possibility of summitting (which is effortful and directional) within an environment that lends itself to effortless and directionless browsing and surfing. On a minimal level, we can see evidence of this in the corralling of browsing into scrolling timelines and harnessed into "liking," both of which give some directionality to the virtually flat features of the internet, allowing one to "learn." In an overtly educational context, this problematic includes everything from the instructional video (as found on YouTube) to more interactive forms of gamification to MOOCs. We are not here to evaluate the success of any of these models. Rather we want to highlight how each model calls for evaluation: an evaluation of how means and ends are conjoined

---

1. The ease of browsing we are discussing is not open and available to all. Indeed, search engines reproduce White privilege and discriminate against women of color through "algorithms of oppression" (Noble, 2018). In this sense, the ideal conditions for browsing are implicitly White, heteronormative, and male.

with relation to certain success conditions. Browsing lacks success conditions. One cannot assess whether one browsed well or surfed well without losing the directionless and effortless wandering that defines the experience of browsing. Learning dictates that the digital *must become* a means to an educational end. In other words, learning must yoke the infinite resources of browsing to a particular end for the purpose of evaluation. If browsing lacks works, learning must force browsing to produce some kind of work that communicates what has been done or achieved, and this means corralling browsing's endlessness toward a specific end.

It is our contention that e-study is different in kind from e-learning. Instead of transforming browsing into summitting, e-study takes up the pure means of the internet and makes the experience of such means educational in and of itself (without uniting it to an end). Once again drawing on Flusser (2014), we would argue that studying is a distinct gesture of education that is without work and does not communicate anything.[2] Because studious gestures do not gesture toward completion of a work, they are, in a sense, *disinterested,* meaning that they are not concerned with ends. And instead of conveying a message to someone else, they circle back around and are ultimately directed at their own activity. In this sense, they are *ritualistic* gestures. A genuine ritual is an "unpractical practice" (124). The unpractical nature of ritual practice means that it is not beholden to the functionality of communication or the concretization of work. It produces nothing beyond its own iteration as a kind of pure means (instead of a means to an end).

Instead of mere browsing, the disinterested and unpractical ritual of studying can be characterized by yet another mode of educational movement: drift. The movement of study as educational drifting is best captured in this brief description of a moment of study offered by Agamben: "Those who are acquainted with long hours spent

2. For a more detailed overview of the relation between Flusser's theory of gestures and study, see Lewis 2019.

roaming among books when every citation, every codex, every initial encountered seems to open a new path, immediately left aside at the next encounter or who have experienced the labyrinthine allusiveness of that 'law of good neighbors' whereby Warburg arranged his library, know that not only can study have no rightful end, but does not even desire one" (1995, 64). In this citation, Agamben highlights how study is not oriented toward ends so much as the experience of moving from one text to the next without closure or completion. Good neighbors in this sense does not mean that every book resembles every other book. Instead, it means that the books—when neighboring each other—evoke thought through abrupt juxtapositions, allegorical connections, unexpected resonances, and so on. One does not know where one is heading as one is drawn into the tangle. Instead, the studier "roams" among citations that emerge between good neighbors. These recursive movements of back and forth drag on for "long hours" in an indeterminate manner, and through this prolongation, there is no clear or easily determined sense of development, growth, or progress. The mention of the labyrinth is important to note. While a maze has an entrance and a separate exit, labyrinths have only one point of entry, and as such are meant to be inescapable. Because of this, one's movements left or right, this way or that, cannot be evaluated in relation to achieving a certain aim. Instead, the movements are simply that: movements without an end to guide them. In the labyrinth, one cannot learn to improve. Instead, one is constantly "stupefied" (64). Stupefaction is itself a vibration or "shuttling between bewilderment and lucidity" (64). In this sense, stupefaction is not a state of not thinking. Rather, it is thinking brought to a halt in front of its own potentiality to think. It is thinking the place (or s-pacing) of thinking. For this reason, one cannot conclude the act of studying as it has no content beyond its own potentiality.

Unlike summitting, the drifting qualities of study lack an end to orient them. Because of this, there are no criteria constituting a completed work or capable of communicating success. Study is, as Agamben describes, endless and stupefying (meaning that it never knows where it is in a course of growth, development, or progress). This makes study sound like it is nothing more than an educational equivalent to internet browsing. Certainly the two share features, but there is an important, though subtle, distinction to be made here. Drift highlights *tension* or what Agamben refers to as a rhythmic *shuttling* between states that provokes stupefying contemplation. To drift, one must yield to the push and pull of a certain flow that is beyond one's control and get taken up by the strange, internal resonances that emerge when forces start to swirl. Here we can turn to Deleuze's appeal to "analysis in terms of movements" (1995b, 121): "All the new sports—surfing, windsurfing, hang-gliding—take the form of entering into an existing wave. There's no longer an origin as starting point, but a sort of putting-into-orbit. The key thing is how to get taken up in the motion of a big wave, a column of rising air, to 'get into something' instead of being the origin of an effort" (121). There is no summit here to stand outside and above the currents. Instead one is always *immersed* in studious drifting. As Deleuze and Guattari (1987) specify, a "line of drift" is composed of "different loops, knots, speeds, movements, gestures, and sonorities" (311–12). To survive, one has to yield to the internal forces that tug and toggle this way and that within the loops of drift. While spatially flat like the space of the internet, the space of drift is restless with various vectors of force that can draw a studier into something only to suddenly be abandoned by an emergent current of thought that intercepts and throws one off course. These currents and tensions provide a minimal structure for study—a minimal force field to hold the uncertainty of study. Think here of Agamben at drift in the library: the ritual of turning and returning to certain books or circling back and forth around a possible topic are not practical (as they delay completion, efficiency, graduation, and so forth), but they are practices that flow through and within the limitations of the library. On our reading the library can be thought of as a *loosely* knotted space and time for studious drift. The "good neighbors" provide the loops and sonorities between ideas, but in such a way as to remain pliable and open for drift to circulate.

Such circular, repetitious drift is not willed. Study is a special kind of yielding to or getting taken up by a big wave. The need to yield (or be utterly fatigued or pulled apart) is not easy, and can send the studier into dangerous territory. As studiers eschew the stability of e-learning structures to embrace more volatile structures that always threaten to destabilize, they can lose their bearings, intentionally so, and risk foundering. Risk, therefore, is integral to studious drift. In this sense, study is an achievement (like learning) but one that lacks a goal and identifiable outcomes (like browsing). Perhaps another way of summarizing these distinctions is as follows: learning is willful, browsing lacks a will, and study is willing (in the sense of disinterested and yielding to a drift, even if it strains).

And finally, study can be thought of as purposive without a purpose. Learning is an example of an educational movement that has both purposiveness and a purpose. The purpose (as final cause) orients the purposiveness of the activity, giving it shape and directionality. Browsing, on the other hand, lacks both purposiveness and purpose. This is precisely why browsing feels like a "waste of time" or a "meaningless" or "frivolous" activity. Drifting is perhaps more paradoxical. We would characterize this kind of movement as releasing purposiveness from any determinate purpose. Certainly studious drift *feels* like it is not meaningless or frivolous. Indeed, for the studier, his or her life might be at stake in the act of study, existentially speaking. Yet such movement is not directed by an overarching purpose. In divorcing purposiveness from purpose-as-final-cause, one also simultaneously relinquishes the need for destinations, so the originating and terminating points associated with the summiting process are replaced with a perpetual unfolding of potentialities. Hence the difficultly of spelling out what has been achieved or where one is heading when one is perpetually caught in the drift of study. Instead, one is more inclined to scratch one's head as if stupefied at where one has been and how one is proceeding. Because one is immersed in the drift—and thus indifferent to ends—one might even get annoyed with pragmatic questions such as, "What work has been produced from all this?" While learning involves the risk of failure and browsing lacks any sense of risk, study involves the risk of *exposing* the self to an activity that cannot be evaluated and in which one might lose one's bearings, dissolving into an activity that, paradoxically, seems to deactivate itself in the moment of stupefaction.

As such, the problematic for e-study is different from that of e-learning. E-learning must *resist* the movement of the medium. Learnification of the internet environment commands the insertion of structures for evaluating progress or regress, thus abruptly halting browsing through means-end directionality. It must implement forms of testing that activate the agency of the will on the part of the learner, so that the learner can develop through the trials and tribulations of summitting. The popular LMS software used by American universities offers a case in point. Such platforms are put in place to establish summiting structures, including dashboards, settings, reports, assignments, gradebooks, and so on. Their intent is to centralize and organize learning mechanisms and achievement indicators, intentionally inhibiting students' ability to browse, as is necessary to yield measurable learning outcomes. The problem is how to make the pure means of the internet educationally useful without inserting an end. How to engage currents so that browsing becomes drifting? This means entering into the flow of the internet through hacking and tinkering (Lewis and Friedrich 2016) in such a way that the movement of the internet is phenomenologically *felt* in a new way—a way that stupefies, that causes thinking to think itself without being captured by the apparently effortless flow of hyperlinks, that opens the internet up for new uses that are not necessarily modulated forms of control. Here we are not referring to hacking in the common sense of gaining access to information without authorization. Rather, hacking means taking up a practice in order to decouple means from ends, thus unleashing uses that might not have been foreseen ahead of time.

This of course is a pataphysical educational question, which, to be answered, demands an ontology of the internet. What is the space and time of the internet? This is not an easy question to answer, as the internet seems to be both a striated, controlled space and a smooth space *simultaneously*. Yet we would propose that both are possible only because the internet taps into and throws into relief the pataphysics of *ethernity*. As introduced in chapter 1, Jarry (1996) describes ethernity as a "circularly mobile" "elastic solid" (104) that is equal parts real and virtual. We are interested in how to produce studios that can act as a skiff for drifting across and between material and immaterial, virtual and actual, striated and smooth faces of postdigital experience. Neither total striation nor smoothness, e-studios willingly embrace the push and pull between the two as a space and time for educational experimentation within the loops and knots of ethernity that continually shift the parameters of when, how, and who can engage in educational experimentation. How then do we create a space-time machine that can willingly enter into the drift? What kind of studio is this?

An example of this can be found in our small-scale experiment called Studio_D. The challenge of Studio_D was to take up digital devices and platforms and suspend or render inoperative the infrastructure that supports e-learning in order to unleash studious use in a postdigital world. In other words, Studio_D attempted to deactivate means-end logics internal to learning through certain forms of drift. For us, this meant finding an alternative to e-learning that was nevertheless still educational. To do so, we had interdisciplinary teams of scholars work together to design protocols or experimental prompts that took up various e-learning platforms and introduced an alternative kind of movement—a shift from summiting that nevertheless does not merely resume browsing. We had participants from diverse, international institutions including the University of North Texas, University of Texas at Dallas, Moore College of Art and Design, Columbia University, Arizona State University, KU Leuven, Aalto University, and Hangzhou Normal University. A variety of disciplines and fields were represented by the protocol teams, including art education, studio art, philosophy of education, curriculum and instruction, curatorial studies, language arts, and cognitive engineering.

Once the protocols were designed, they were then posted on the Studio_D website and opened up for experimentation. Teams of students and professors at the aforementioned colleges and universities designated a specific week in the spring of 2020 to complete as many of the protocols as possible. The "results" were then housed on the Studio_D website to be shared publicly. Currently, the website is still active, with hopes that others might take up the protocols and continue the experiments and that more protocols will be added in the future.

At this point we turn toward several of these experiments, grouping them in terms of specific modes of studious drift. Of course, these modes are not perfectly distinct categories, as once a particular drift is set in motion, it has a tendency to spin off into other modes. Instead, the following are pliable (like the space-time machine of the studio itself) and open to contamination and combination with other drifts.

Glitchy Drift

Several participants produced protocols that intentionally hacked into and tinkered with the functionality of basic, taken-for-granted e-learning formats. The key here is to produce protocols that first and foremost render inoperative the metaphysics of learning that are inscribed within certain digital platforms and formats. Such dismantling is, as we explore more fully in the final chapter of this book, anarchic suspension of the laws underlying the instruments, processes, and categories of e-learning. One example is the following protocol designed by Joris Vlieghe and Nancy Vansieleghm titled "Knowledge Clips." The background for the protocol is simple. As Vlieghe and Vansieleghm write:

> The backdrop against which we propose the following protocol is the difficulty not to respond to the request by many universities today to create digital educational resources on demand, and more specifically to create online learning materials that are fully catered to individual students' needs and learning trajectories. In our own university, to be more specific, lecturers are expected to provide

short video fragments (literally translated: "knowledge clips") to students, as this is believed to be a powerful and up-to-date learning resource.

The authors then hacked into the knowledge clip format—thus suspending the ends of learning—in the following way:

> With the help of your own digital devices (smartphone, laptop, etc.), make a *six-minute-long* knowledge clip about precisely one *well-defined* topic, concept or principle. This video should be as *concise* and clear as possible and deal with a subject you deem important and *relevant*. This video can be posted on the conference website or on YouTube so that it can be publicly streamed.
> It is required that:
>
> **1.** Instead of avoiding or minimizing noise/interference, your "knowledge clip" should *explicitly seek out noise/interference*
> **2.** This clip should *avoid* addressing the student-viewer in any *direct* way or *personal* manner
> **3.** Making full use of the specific features of videos, you should *avoid* that the video straightforwardly leads to a *thorough processing* of the offered content

Before discussing implications of this protocol, here is one more example titled "Sounds Like Education" submitted by Sebastian Schlecht, Tomi Slotte Dufva, Taneli Tuovinen, Juuso Tervo, and Annika Sohlman. As they explain it,

> This protocol explores sounds and silences as educational media, focusing specifically on the educational aspects of sound recording.
> In education, sound recordings may be used to support or replace note-taking, to verify what was said during class, or, in case the listener was not present in the lecture, to distribute teaching beyond the confinements of the physical classroom. In other words, they function as tools of remembrance and distribution—two activities that have close ties to the history of education. Recordings are also political. In the U.S., some conservative groups encourage students to record their "liberal" professors in order to "expose" their ideological basis.
> However, speech is but one sound of education. The other sounds—the sound of the room, of the furniture, of bodies moving and acting—constitutes the very milieu, a soundscape, where educa-

tion takes place. How, then, to remember and distribute this milieu? What could we learn from it, what would it mean to study it?

The resulting protocol consisted of the following steps:

1. Record—with a phone, laptop, or a digital recorder—10 minutes of any lecture you're attending.
2. With the help of editing software (such as Audacity [open source]), remove all spoken words from the file. Coughs, laughs, mumbling, etc., may be left.
3. Give the file a title that tells what the lecture was about and submit your manipulated recording.

In both cases, notice the movement here from summitting to drifting. The typical knowledge clip or sound recording is outcome oriented and views digital technology as an instrument (means) for achieving a desired (learning) end. Technology is a mere tool to be used to accomplish a task or gain a certain kind of knowledge. Yet these protocols interrupt or suspend this implicit logic of learning *using the very technological infrastructure meant to achieve an end to subvert such ends*. In other words, they do not negate or destroy the knowledge clip or the recorded lecture, but rather deactivate the metaphysics of learning founding the logic of functionality. When means are released from ends, drift sets in. Drift, in this specific sense, is not unlike the pataphysics of *détournement* first theorized and put into practice by the Situationist International through which infrastructure was rendered inoperative and then put to new artistic use (Debord 2006, 15). In our case, one is no longer oriented toward learning outcomes so much as around the implicit educational atmosphere or technological infrastructure that support learning. The viewer suddenly becomes aware of the media, which is no longer merely a transparent conveyer of information to be learned. Watching or listening to these clips and recordings, one asks, "What aesthetic possibilities are excluded when technology functions according to predefined ends?" or "What is not heard when I listen to the teacher?" In such cases, the situation opens up to drifting away from the means-end metaphysics of learning embodied in the voice and actions of the teacher and supported through technological tools for promoting efficient learning. A drift sets in that reconfigures the glitch less as an obstacle to learning and more as an aesthetic event that has potentials to knot together new speeds and gestures, new forms of distraction and attention, new postdigital forms of awareness of how technological infrastructure has become a transparent and taken-for-granted aspect of educational life in general.

Because of the nature of these hacked clips, the intention to learn on the part of the viewer cannot be consummated. The viewer's will cannot overcome the interference of the medium (bad editing, distorted audio, and poor videography) in order to reach its end (mount the summit). The hacked clips demand that a detour be taken that drifts the learner away from learning to consider more or less "extraneous" details or "annoying" failures. While such clips might be quickly dismissed if they were posted on YouTube as "useless" or "pointless" (inevitably receiving poor reviews from those eager to learn), within Studio_D, they trigger a specific kind of study on the part of the audience. Drift is induced in the viewer, who is suddenly caught up in a current of content that leads nowhere in particular; lessons do not seem to teach anything; outcomes are conclusively inconclusive; practices are impractical, and yet there is nevertheless a sense of purposiveness propelling the clips even if this purposiveness does not generate knowledge.

Induced glitches are therefore breakdowns in the use of technological infrastructure that open them up to alternative forms of educational life that drift away from learning, but in doing so, open up moments of surprising pleasure in the unexpectedness of a detour. Algorithmic manipulation would be another way to produce glitchy drift, one that is much more structural in nature, disrupting the encoding of learning in terms of computational infrastructure that supports e-learning apps and environments. It is important to note that such algorithmic glitches would not simply destroy or adapt to their various logics of control, but rather suspend the connections between means-end educational metaphysics and the executability of code in order to open up new use through algorithmic alchemy.

Iterative Drift

Another mode of drift we would like to call "iterative." Here, the linear logic of learning that leads from teacher to student, from input to output, from distribution to assessment is interrupted, creating circular, seemingly endless recursive patterns. If the communicative logic of learning concerns a simple economic exchange between teacher and student (Biesta 2006), wherein the teacher verifies what has been received through an assessment, iterative drift creates a diagonal line of flight away from this verification, producing various vortexes and eddies that no longer lead *toward* (another outcome) so much as *back* to the very preconditions of educational communication as such. One such protocol is WeChat/WeiXin, written by Hu Jun and Christopher Moffett. The background of the protocol is described as follows:

> As one possible entrance into the following para-educational protocol, we might simply evoke what Paulo Freire calls "the great achievement of Gabriel Bode." Bode's great contribution was to solve the recurring impasse of people failing to decode a singular politically-compressed image, by showing next to it a variety of other "auxiliary" images that would keep the conversation from lapsing into silence. From image, via images, to spoken words.
>
> We should recall, however, that the sonorous, for Freire, is linked to banking education, where inputs match outputs. So is it that the image—or of great necessity, that mother of invention—images, trouble the too facile, or too silent, mouth?
>
> Without answering this, let us throw up another image, next to that of this sonorous bank. The term, familiar in German, that is translated as "Nuremberg Funnel" can be traced back, at least, to Georg Philipp Harsdörffer. It suggests a mechanical aid to learning that funnels knowledge through the head or mouth. But what is of interest is that in the baroque Europe of 1647, Harsdörffer evokes this image in a work entitled *Poetic funnel: The art of German poetry and rhyme, without*

using the Latin language, poured in VI hours. In this work on poetry, Harsdörffer explores a mechanical, combinatory practice for producing poetry that involves laying different words up against each other in order to computationally evoke latent poetic effects.

The protocol has no comment on this juxtaposition. It simply attempts to produce, within a fixed number of hours, a combinatory effect of images and poetry, be it as it may.

The authors then suggest the following protocol:

One Week in Advance
1. Email to potential participants with invitation.

Three Days in Advance
1. Participants install WeChat on their phones, and add the coordinators as contacts.
2. Participants are arranged in a cycle, alternating as much as possible between native languages.
3. Each participant is connected with the next participant in the cycle as a contact, and accepts the connection of someone else in turn.

First Hour (Morning, Central; Evening, China)
1. Each participant chooses a 3″ × 4″ vertical, found or made image (copyright free), and sends it in a chat to the next participant.
2. Each participant combines the image they sent and the image they received into a horizontal diptych, with their image on the left.
3. Each participant sends this diptych to the next participant, along with the original image they received.

Ongoing for the next 47 Hours
1. Upon receiving a diptych (with single image), participants compose a one-to-two-line poem in response to the diptych, and forward it to the next participant, along with the single image they received.
2. Upon receiving a poem (with single image), they are to add a new image to the image received, that responds to the poem as translated by We Chat, creating a new diptych. This diptych, as well as the received image, are passed to the next participant.

Upon Completion
1. Individual threads will be shared to Group Thread of all participants. A discussion of the process can follow in the thread.

In this protocol, the space-time of the studio takes on a certain circular, almost labyrinthian quality. Recall that for Agamben, the library-as-studio is not so much a maze as a labyrinth that is organized according to the "law of good neighbors" wherein each book suggests a lead, thread, clue, or drift that sets in motion the loops of contemplation. Likewise with WeChat/WeiXin, word and image merge and diverge in such a way as to continually repotentialize the act of communication. Something new can always emerge from within the repetition through the tiniest of drifts. The native translation feature in WeChat further extends and intensifies the poetic variability of language, often leading to inscrutable or surprising drifts. This, in turn, creates the preconditions for the contemplation of the potentiality of communication as such, or the *communicability* that lies not at the end of any act of communicating ("message received") so much as with experimentation with the means of communicative iteration as such.

Parodic Drift

Another mode of drift is captured in the protocol titled "Self(study) ies." Originally inspired equally by the photographs of studio spaces (as images of potentiality) presented by Agamben in his book *Autoritratto nello Studio* (2017) as well as the work of photographer Ian Wallace, who turned the camera toward his own studio space, Tyson E. Lewis and James Thurman created "Self(study) ies." Throughout his many books, Agamben has demonstrated a consistent fascination with images that reveal their potentiality without putting it to work, such as Diego Velázquez's famous *Las Meninas* (1656) in which the painter paints himself painting, thus manifesting the potentiality to paint in the painting itself. The same can be said for Agamben's images of the humble studios he has used over his lifetime: these are images that turn thought away from the content of thought toward the act of thinking, the potentiality to think (thinkability, or the infrastructure supporting the gesture of thinking). Wallace utilizes a similar approach in his photographs of studios but perhaps with the reverse intent: not to depict the potentiality of actuality but rather the actuality of potentiality! In both cases, images of studios take the internal, individual capacity for revery and contemplation and ultimately turn outward, revealing its own possibility.

In "Self(study)ies," Lewis and Thurman offer a studious parody of the selfie. They write,

> Selfies usually are forms of personal branding or personal image crafting to convey the message of living up to expectations of a successful, beautiful, productive, exciting, fulfilling life. For this protocol, we want to hack into and render inoperative the function of the selfie turning it into a self(study)ie, or a self-portrait of you as a studier.

The protocol that follows is summarized in two simple moves:

> **1.** Produce an image of you studying and/or your equipment for study. It ought to capture moments of intense study, or moments of free time when playing with materials or ideas becomes possible, when the expectations for productivity and efficiency are left idle, when individuals put a pause on their outcomes-based learning in order to take time to get lost, repeat themselves, wander, stumble upon a question when an individual experiences create intellectual vertigo, and when the impulse to do busy-work is suspended, unleashing another rhythm to educational life.
>
> **2.** Write about what you see in the self(study)ies. What does the image reveal about the conditions that make study possible for you as a studier? Think about contextual (time, place, objects), physical (rest, relaxation, or tension), and psychological (mood) conditions that the image reveals.

Lewis and Thurman hack into the format and function of the selfie in order to create a parody of a taken-for-granted trope in contemporary, digital culture. Parody, in this sense, remains close to the original but with a slight difference that somehow renders the intended meaning or function of the original inoperative. It is a profanation of the original that opens it up for new uses that subvert expectations. If selfies promote self-commodification (the self as image spectacle), then self(study)ies parodically pick up this common form of self-objectification and open it up for study. The resulting images are not sexy or romantic or interesting or exciting. They are quiet, almost silent meditations on a self thinking its own possibility through the objects of its thinking. This strange moment is the precise point of contact when subject and object distinctions seem to collapse, inside becomes outside, and potentiality and actuality mix without one extinguishing the other. The result is an image of the self at the precise moment when it disappears into its own potentiality.

In the spring of 2020, this protocol became particularly interesting as it was a moment when schools and universities were moving online and out of classrooms. Everyone was reconfiguring rooms, beds, closets, nooks, and crannies as temporary "studios." Studioing thus made various spaces within the house into spaces adjacent, small pockets of potentiality carved out from the utility and functionality of household spaces for the sometimes-inoperative ritual of study to take place. The images and memories captured in "Self(study)ies" is a record of this awkward, postdigital moment when questions of studioing suddenly became urgent in the face of shutdowns and lockdowns, provoking experimentations with a reconfiguration of the relationship between the solitary self and the virtual community, between the operative space and time of the household and the inoperative space and time of study, between distance and nearness, between inside and outside.

Citational Drift

If we conceptualize an essay as a closed system with a beginning, a middle, and an end, then the citation is almost like a space adjacent to the text from within the text yet beyond the text. It is a tiny drift within the text that opens up the text to its outside. The "law of good neighbors" induces citational drift across, between, and within texts. This strange capacity of citations to lead the reader astray from the text that they are a/part of was eloquently captured by Kim Lesley, Maya Pindyck, and Daniel Tucker in their protocol "One Sentence Research Paper, Reiterated." Their protocol is described as:

1. To prompt different modes of digital research that facilitate critiques of existing systems of categorization/naming.
2. To explore where different selections, condensations, and assemblages of language can take us.
3. To engage search constraints as a mode of research.

This threefold intention was operationalized in terms of the following protocol steps:

1. Create a one sentence research "paper" stating a topic of interest. Think of the sentence as a distilled and condensed abstract.
2. Then, do any number of the following prompts, depending on how you see them relating to your particular project:
   - Hyperlink each word in your sentence to digital resources constrained by a library's database.
   - Hyperlink each word in your sentences to YouTube content only.
   - Hyperlink each work to any internet source (website, video, article, image, etc.).

If you do more than one, observe the differences created by each constraint. What do you notice? What has this exercise suggested to you about the power of framing? What about the power of sequencing? What about research practices? How is language used to organize information in the digital contexts you engaged? How do we—or can we—interface with controlled vocabularies in our research processes?

If you only do one, observe differences across peer creations. Take the sentence you wrote and experiment with rewriting it three different ways. Explore informational ways of re-iterating the sentence as well as more poetic, surrealist, or literary ways. Hyperlink each word in each of those sentences to any digital resources. Consider where language can take us and how it affects constructions of knowledge.

Like Drucker's pataphysically inspired speculative computing experiments (2009), this protocol is an attempt to suspend the rather mechanistic approach to data organization and retrieval found in entity-driven approaches to knowledge and to foreground principles of subjectivity, emergence, contingency, complexity, multiperspectivalism, and heteroglossia. Taking up Drucker's lead, this protocol pushes the boundaries of what counts as research by inverting the typical proportionality between text and citation. Here, citation overtakes the text. The outside effectively becomes the inside; the marginalia becomes the message! If the citation is a manifestation of the potentiality of the text making itself present (without exhausting itself), then here the potentiality overtakes the actuality of the text without negating or destroying the text. Instead, the radical potentialization of the actual text sets the text adrift. Unlike traditional hyperlinked browsing, the minimal structure provided by the research sentence institutes the law of good neighbors, which always orients the links back to the question of the potentiality left within the text that has yet to be developed. Instead of a definitive meaning (supported by citations) that one can learn from, or an endless array of meaningless digressions in which meaning is always delayed or deferred (nothing but hyperlinks that lose their citational reference point), the research sentence as conceptualized in this protocol offers a constantly renewed experience of *potential* meaning (through the implosion of text and citation). These are citations that *don't work* or prefer not to work as citations within the structure of the text. The text does not summit the citation (forcing it to work), and the citation does not destroy the text through an endless stream of browsing. Instead, the text-as-citation and citation-as-text always drift back to the studious question of the meaningful nature of communication's indeterminacy displaying itself (a communication that communicates nothing beyond its own communicability).

As Drucker summarizes: the effects of speculative computing conduced at SpecLab "serve as an example of work that began without any clear outcome, highly risky and much laughed at—only to be realized and recognized as useful in fact as well as concept" (2009, 35–36). Pataphysical experimentation in and through postdigital studioing risks ridicule as "pointless" precisely because it is! Drift has no point (or rather, points cannot contain or modulate the direction of lines). It is an unpractical practice, as Flusser would say. Yet there is an underlying sense of purposiveness for those caught up in the drift, a unique kind of pleasure that accompanies one along the path of the detour (which of course never actually gets someone to the original destination). This might be laughable for those constrained by the metaphysics of learning, but for the studier, it is as stupefying as it is edifying.

At this point, it is important to highlight the unique features of Studio_D as a *space* that induces modes of drifting. Unlike e-learning, which is a structured space (think of the knowledge clip or Canvas homepages), or the internet, which is completely unstructured, flat, and purely rhizomatic (think here of hyperlinks), Studio_D is a platform containing the protocols that knot together ideas, gestures, speeds, objects ("good neighbors"), and so forth into a situation of study. Study traces out the twists and turns in the knots. Thus the structure of the studio is the structure of the knot. Protocols interacting with ideas and bodies produce resonances that push and pull. Instead of spiraling *out* as with browsing, or *up* as in summitting, the studier drifts further and further *into* the experiments induced by the protocols. In the case of Studio_D, loose, minimal infrastructure to support the experimentation involved a basic website housing a project statement, the protocols themselves, and the resulting material manifestations of study. Whereas e-learning spaces might be thought of as mazes to be navigated through in order to "win," Studio_D is configured as a labyrinth, which is a closed, finite space (a neighborhood of references and resources that loop toward and away from one another) that is nevertheless endless, circular, and, for these reasons, generative for studious drifting.

Likewise, we can think of the time of studious drift as introducing a *temporal* de-completion of learning. It is a slow haste. Whereas browsing is pure haste (quick and effortless time) and learning is slow, willful perseverance, drifting is a pataphysical time *between*. Viewers of Studio_D watch, puzzled; they are pulled in (against their will to learn) and linger on strange images and activities that seem to suspend the ends that are assumed to accompany any "legitimate" educational enterprise. Suddenly, they are adrift in a space and time adjacent to learning—under it, behind it, above it, or to the side of it. And in these anomalous, limbo-like spaces, there is a sense of rhythmic swaying back and forth to the point where progress and regress lose all meaning, and one is instead left with the sensation that *something is happening but it is impossible to evaluate it or calculate its duration*. One falls off the clock. Temporality ceases to be unidirectional, neutral, or homogenous and instead becomes circular, meandering, indeterminate. This sensation is the temporal manifestation of the potentiality of the ritual turning and returning of disinterested study that studioing makes possible. Both enacting and viewing the protocols in Studio_D reveal a pataphysical educational experiment with and through time, or an experiment that is active through an unpractical and dispassionate practice that only "produces" solutions if they remain imaginary. Perhaps we can say that these are spatial and temporal anomalies of ethernity effecting the gravity of learning as a dominant educational practice. Like dark matter and energy, the ripples of ethernity produce aberrations in the space-time continuum, causing drifts to happen.

In sum, Studio_D refers equally to a digital studio and studio drift. They come hand in hand. Stated differently, studioing taps into and maximizes the educational potentials that are unique to the ethernity of postdigital techno-cultural-educational contacts without collapsing this potentiality into mere browsing. And the cultivation of such studious drift is particularly meaningful in the face of events that unmoor societies, such as the coronavirus pandemic. Educational logics that have been taken for granted are suddenly put under great stress. Physical, intellectual, and virtual spaces are reconfigured. Normal modes of human interaction are problematized. Addressing these issues cannot be done through means-end directionality alone. As studious drift is risk-oriented, it provides an avenue for the development of experimental, imaginary solutions and intrepid thinking. In this sense, digital space-time machines such as Studio_D might offer an alternative to e-learning spaces, and they do so by experimenting with the educational use of postdigital means. Such experimentation is paramount, given the push toward increasing levels of online education that will most likely follow the coronavirus pandemic. In this sense, the pandemic is offering a challenge and an opportunity to think differently about what higher education might look and feel like beyond the metaphysics of learning and its spatialization and temporalization in the form of the brick-and-mortar classroom.

3. Protocols as Experimental Writing for the Studio

WHEN ONE THINKS of the university professor's work, one immediately is drawn to the practice of lecturing. Indeed, lecturing and the university seem to be synonymous. Depictions of medieval universities focus on the professor reading a book to a gathering of students who, in turn, attempt to copy the text as closely as possible. University practice has, for centuries, focused on dictation and/or note-taking in relation to the lecture. Critics of this practice have noticed how insufficient lecturing has become for conveying the complexity of contemporary knowledge production and distribution, and have called for its replacement as a way of rehabilitating an ailing university system (Laurillard 2002). We agree in part with this critique but see it largely as misplaced. What critics of lecturing are actually concerned with is not lecturing as such so much as with how lecturing has come to embody the metaphysics of learning as a simple, unilateral transmission and dissemination model of education akin to school-like teaching (Masschelein and Simons 2013, 113). While it is certainly true that lecturing can and does embody such a metaphysical commitment, this does not mean that the pliability of lecturing weds it necessarily to learning. Instead, learning has appropriated lecturing as a convenient form (often misunderstanding its pataphysical movements).

Bearing this in mind, we highlight several underappreciated dimensions of lecturing that are missed by its critics. In particular, we would like to shift focus from the *formal* qualities of lecturing to the implied *movements* that lecturing induces. First, during the middle ages, lecturing was not so much about transmitting knowledge so much as reproducing texts in the form of the dictation of books or the transcription of a lecturer's commentary by students acting as scribes. These acts of copying resulted in "drifting texts and vanishing manuscripts" (Eisenstein 1997, 114). Lecturing thus enabled the drift of texts in two senses, first vertically from generation to generation and second horizontally throughout the lecture hall and beyond. It is this drifting notion of lecturing that connects lecturing up to a certain pataphysical notion of educational life that always butts up against any law of order that dictates who can do what when and where.[1]

Second, lecturing can be thought of less as a stubborn return to oral culture than as a practice of "intermediality" (Freisen 2011) embodying a negotiation between (perhaps competing) media. For the medieval professor, this meant that lecturing translated visual language into an auditory form. Lecturing was literally reading out loud, enabling the written word to be heard (and thus copied directly by students). Later, romantic intellectuals utilized the educational form of the lecture to verbalize the otherwise inaudible sound/presence of the genius or spirit of the lecturer. And more recently, the lecture (more or less liberated from the verbatim textual recital) makes appear the sound of the lecturer's inner thoughts for the audience through an enactment of thinking (even if this enactment is an illusion of spontaneous, fresh talk). Today, lecturing has become even more adaptable, proving itself to be a potent educational form

---

1. It is important to note that Masschelein and Simons (2011) describe the university in terms of various "experimental movements" of profanation rather than institutional crystallizations. It is not the lecture that is essential to the university but rather the movement that it embodies, a movement that we describe as drift (as a profanation of the sacred in order to produce knots and loops between people, things, and ideas).

for mediating between texts, graphics, and gestures in a postdigital world. Intermediality thus enables us to posit yet another form of drift that characterizes the lecture: a drift across and through various forms of media, both dispersing itself while also acting as an educational nexus capable of holding together words, sounds, images, bodies, and screens. That which is visually read can come to be heard, that which is heard can come to be seen, that which is internal can be made external, and that which is virtual can be made actual.

Third, as Lavinia Marin, Jan Masschelein, and Maarten Simons argue (2018), a lecture is an act of profaning sacred texts by making them public or common. The quintessential gesture of the university is precisely such profanation. As lecturing became less tethered to specific texts and was reconceptualized as an act of thinking out loud, thinking became a *performance* in front of an active audience of note-takers. Thinking as inner monologue gave way to the commons. Like the lecture itself, notes are a profanation of sorts in that they are never direct transcriptions but also contain within themselves a certain amount of drift. Expanding on this point, we can argue that the drift induced by lecturing is a particularly *educational* form of profanation of texts and thoughts as they are set in motion and dispersed through mediatic displacements and public performance.

Finally, it is interesting to note that in *A Thousand Plateaus*, Deleuze and Guattari recount a rather surreal lecture given by Arthur Conan Doyle's character Professor Challenger, in which the lecturer appears to drift into an altered state. They write, "You still couldn't put your finger on it, but Challenger seemed to be deterritorializing on the spot" (1987, 64). The act of lecturing sets in motion a certain drift *within* the lecturer. In Professor Challenger's case, this meant that lecturing caused a change in his voice, appearance, and tone that were hard to describe but nevertheless were distinctive alterations in his comportment. Thus lecturing ruptures habituated or sedimented forms of the self, opening up the self to drift in new directions. In this sense, to lecture is to fundamentally risk the self and recognition of the self as *a* self. Lecturing is an experiment on the self by the self in relation to a public.

In this chapter, we do not seek to either save the lecture nor destroy it. Rather we ask two questions: First, how can the essential movement of lecturing as a form of educational drift be intensified and expanded? Second, how would this enable the pataphysical dimensions of lecturing to free themselves for new educational uses beyond the metaphysics of learning? To answer these questions, we might very well have to jettison the historically recognizable form of the lecture as such in order to hold onto and pay tribute to the kind of pataphysical and postdigital drift that it sets in motion. In short, we have to let the drift of lecturing drift away from itself. And with this drift, at the very dissipation of the form of the lecture, we find ourselves at the threshold of the studio as a space-time machine a-part from the university and its lecture halls. Here we can recall how studioing takes up drift and overtly thematizes and induces it through a-disciplinary, a-topic experimentation without the need to be tethered to a text or orator or lecture hall. While this might appear to be the antithesis of lecturing, it is our contention that such experimentation in the space-time opened up and sustained by studioing is actually an intensification and extension of the pataphysics of studious drift found in the intermediality of the lecture, and in this sense, is more true to the profanatory movement of the university than many versions of lecturing found today that appear to embody a metaphysics of learning.

But if this is the case, then what kind of preparatory writing is needed to sustain the space and time of such studious drift? What kind of writing can create the *situation* of studioing (as a knotting and a looping together)? Traditionally, the lecturer recited a text, or read glosses on texts, or performed thought with the aid of notes. Throughout, practices of reading, writing, and thinking (not always in that order) form the preparatory work of the teacher, lecturer, or professor. In this chapter, we will argue that protocoling is a unique kind of preparatory writing that emerges out of and in constant dialogue with drifting. It is less a text, gloss, or set of notes than it is a minimal procedural outline for generating the possibility of study through a common space-time of the studio. It does not rest on the authority of the text or the presence of the self as a source. Instead, it displaces the text even further while simultaneously compromising the idea of a self as source (of spirit, knowledge, or simply information). And in this sense, the protocol as a new kind of writing wrestles the movement of drift away from the structures and forms of the lecture that lend it to cooptation by learning as its definitive, institutional form.

The word "protocol" is particularly apt for describing this kind of writing, especially in relation to e-study in the sense that computer science also uses the term. But we will chart a rather different genealogy for protocoling that is decisively a-disciplinary, a-topic, impractical, and pataphysical in that it refuses to lend itself to standardized learning conditions, opting instead for the singular situations of studioing. Our protocols will not fulfill computational functions so much as intercept them for new use beyond the economy of learning management. In this sense, our protocols do not represent more effective e-learning instruments than lectures (thus replacing lectures with preferable means for achieving the ends of learning). Instead, they are perhaps *less* effective if not downright ineffective for enhanced learning, but only in so far as they open up alternative pataphysical dimensions of experience beyond learning. In conclusion, we will offer a set of loose constraints defining the unproductive and unpragmatic (in)operativity of the protocol (as illustrated in the previous chapter).

The Protocol

The following is a brief genealogy of the protocol (as we have theorized and employed it in our practice). It is not a genetic genealogy that implies a filiation of inheritances. Instead, it ought to be read as a meandering, rhizomatic drift that puts singularities derived from science, art, and literature in relation to one another. The resulting cryptogenealogy is underground, feral, and historically irresponsible, yet nevertheless makes the outline of the protocol intelligible as a particular kind of writing practice. The task of the genealogy is to simultaneously intensify and extend the drift of the lecture while also using the profanatory nature of the lecture to make common the more esoteric and occultist dimensions of the protocol's other, subterranean influences. Moreover, it helps to demonstrate how recklessness is a condition necessary to the generation of the protocol and related experimentation, as well as the guiding ethos of studious drift.

The Secret Recipe

The first inspiration for our concept of the protocol is the literature of secrets in the middle ages. As William Eamon writes (1994), books of secrets were compilations of recipes, formulas, and experiments drawn from various crafts. In the twelfth century, alchemical texts translated into Latin from Arabic sources outlining both practical experimental formulae and esoteric theory concerning the transmutation and ennobling of metals joined with the medieval literature of secrets tradition (Principe 2013). Although largely forgotten today, we can still draw inspiration from this defunct literary form in several respects. First, unlike modern science and its interest in generalizable laws, the books of secrets were more or less concerned with the marvelous, miraculous, and the exceptional (*meraviglia*). They offered catalogues of the irregular rather than the regular functions of nature. For instance, Giambattista Della Porta's book *Magia Naturalis* (1589) was a book of "natural magic" for investigating the extraordinary. On our reading, such books were a kind of pre-pataphysical writing invested in the study of states of exception and singularities. Second, rather than antiscience, these texts existed on a threshold of indistinction between religion and science. They were, in other words, a-disciplinary, crossing boundaries between the occult and the scientific, the ritualistic and the experimental, craft traditions and revelation. For instance, although alchemical recipes overtly concerned the making and counterfeiting of gold, on a deeper level, they covertly concerned the mystical possibility of resurrection. Third, unlike scientific texts of today, which emphasize clarity and transparency in writing, books of secrets often reveled in obscure emblems, allegories, exaggerations, and hidden correspondences. It would be too easy to dismiss this convention hiding ignorance and experimental ineptitude behind a veil of mysticism. Rather, books of secrets partook in the early modern obsession with deciphering riddles and allegories as a serious intellectual practice (Praz 1975). Thus these strange books combined scholastic and experimental elements in often times bizarre constellations that suggest hidden connections or *discordia concors* (harmonious discord) that have to be deciphered through ritualistic reading, experimenting, rereading, more experimenting, and so forth. Existing before clear divisions and separations partitioned out fields of knowledge, methodological specializations, and discursive specifications, books of secrets pointed toward a possible alternative (pataphysical) path. Finally, books of secrets did not abide by conventional academic standards and were skeptical of academic authorities. Those who compiled the books were just as likely to consult with housewives, farmers, or empirics for recipes. Thus the books promoted the drift of recipes across social strata and opened up a space of contamination between empirical and scholastic, legitimate and illegitimate forms of study.[2]

While many of the recipes were immanently practical—dealing with everyday problems—the tradition did not merely concern pragmatic applications. For instance, the examples of actual texts that survive show little evidence of wear and tear that would come about in a workshop or kitchen. This trivial detail seems to indicate that the books were both literary compositions and pseudoscientific manuals that could just as easily be contemplated as they could be enacted. Furthermore, many of the experiments proved to be impossible. While historians such as Eamon see this as something of a drag on the development of modern science, we would make another point. The aim was not always to *learn* a skill (in order to

2. For an example of a contemporary, postdigital book of secrets, see Rasmi and Schildermans 2021.

become an accomplished artisan or solve an immanent problem) but also to *study* the texts as repositories of impossible solutions and hidden signatures existing between singularities. The texts opened themselves up to drift (as they were often arranged idiosyncratically and anachronistically and were full of juxtapositions that promoted labyrinthian allusions) and set drift in motion (as the mind moved through the multiple recipes, riddles, archaic imagery, and their implied resonances). The secrets crossed essential boundaries, invoked provocations, contaminated reason, opened pathways to the absurd, and sought to harmonize the incongruent—all of which provoke unpractical study rather than practical learning.

We want to hold onto these features of the books of secrets while, at the same time, open up the secrets to the drift of commoning and profanation. The problem with the literature of secrets is that it remained bound to a notion of the sacred that had to be protected by the initiates from contamination by the general population. The irony here is clear: these books set in motion the dispersal (drift) of esoteric recipes while at the same time attempting to conceal the covert religious dimensions of such recipes through hidden ciphers and allegories that only the initiates would have access to. For instance, in the Latin West, philosophical and theological contexts might have been lost for many of the alchemical recipes found in books of secrets, yet the recipes collected by figures such as Della Porta became "sacred" property meant for princely eyes only. But how can we take up the idea of the recipe and make it common? One such attempt was the *comici ciarlatani* in early modern Europe, who took recipes from the books of secrets and performed them in public. Somewhere between folk healers, street entertainers, court jesters, and entrepreneurs, we find in the *comici ciarlatani* an ambiguous point where esoteric secrets became common without reassurances of legitimization by an academic institution (as is the case with university lecturers). And yet, even here, we discover a serious problem. While the charlatans were able to make esoteric secrets common, their own authority (or desire for power) prevented them from encouraging audiences to experiment in the production of exceptions. We want the protocol to encourage the generation of profane secrets rather than the mere circulation of existing secrets. What does this mean? First, the profane secret would no longer be the private property of an elite class. These would be secrets that give themselves away, thus intensifying and extending the drifting already at work in the books of secrets. Second, they would not be secrets to be worshiped or simply accepted based on supposed authority or sacredness. Instead, they would be secret recipes for *use,* to be used, and thus experimented with. Third, they would be secrets that resist divisions between science and art, knowledge and taste, scholasticism and empiricism, thus holding firm to a pataphysical, alternative possibility that suspends and renders inoperative the terminology used to define modes of inquiry in the university today.

Impossible Machine Blueprints

The second inspiration comes from Jarry himself. In particular, we are referring to Jarry's blueprint for a time machine. Jarry's blueprint can be considered a protocol for fundamentally altering the space-time coordinates of average everyday experience. The proposed machine is difficult to imagine, but perhaps we can read the plan differently as a blueprint for the studio itself as a space-time machine. For instance, the main component of Jarry's argument is as follows, "If we could lock ourselves inside a Machine that isolates us from Time (except for the small and normal 'speed of duration' that will stay with us because of inertia), all future and past instances could be explored successively, just as the stationary spectator of a panorama has the illusion of a swift voyage through a series of landscapes" (2013, 4). The studio provides isolation from the functional time of everyday life. It takes one out of the flow of events, and in this sense is a special kind of suspension of action. Through an isolation from the stream of events, the events can be studied as if a series of voyages through a landscape. Isolation from action makes the traveler "transparent" to phenomena, allowing them to "pass through us without modifying or displacing us" (5). Slowing down is not stopping. It is rather a fundamental alteration of habitual duration carried in bodies. Jarry describes the work of the Machine as akin to "the viscosity of a liquid" (5), a certain kind of slow haste that is ritualistic in its repetitious, and almost imperceptible, movement (that is nevertheless accelerating).

The resulting Machine can be constructed using the following paradoxical rules. First, it must be rigid and elastic at the same time. Second, it ought to have weight enough to remain stationary while at the same time be incapable of falling. Third, it must be composed of the "perfect elastic solid" (6) or luminiferous ether (ethernity) that enables the Machine to penetrate and be penetrated by any physical body without effect and to circulate without rotation. When properly constructed, the Machine enables travel into the future and the past, producing its own (invisible) present (that is not fully on any timeline, yet not completely outside of it either). It is our argument that Jarry's patamachine is none other than the space-time of the studio itself as a paradoxical location inside and outside the present. The Machine is apart from that which it is a part of. Likewise, its s-pacing makes it untimely. Such paradoxes are compounded when we take into account that the Machine is neither here nor there and neither present nor absent, much like the studio itself as a virtual chamber that remains adjacent.

Blueprints for such a studio are never more than an impossible solution, or a solution that, from within the metaphysics of learning, solves nothing at all (and in this sense is functionless to the economization of learning). Pataphysical blueprints are designs for spaces of experimentation that take up no space, that open a gap in place where things, events, discourses, and practices can be taken up and studied (with a certain indifference to their destinies, functions, or ends).

Artistic Test-Pieces

In describing the studio practice of Eva Hesse, Briony Fer (2004) highlights the importance of test-pieces. Fer interprets these test-pieces as material "notebooks" or commentaries on larger works. But they were more than mere prototypes. Instead, the test-pieces themselves had an autonomous life of their own, often being gathered in glass cases and displayed. These displays, not unlike cabinets of wonder, created strange new connections between bizarre shapes and materials that, when viewed together (as good neighbors), threw into relief Hesse's esoteric practice—a history of experiments. As such, they were not merely means to another end, but rather a meditation on the means of art-making as such—its risks and uncertainties but also its potentialities. As Fer summarizes, "As test-pieces, in which she tried out techniques, they are remnants of her process of making, which are kept and displayed and recycled. The small pieces with which Hesse experimented were highly provisional, yet they come to look like leftovers, especially, of course, as some of the materials, like the latex, have decayed" (34). At first, mere prototypes, in the end, test-pieces leave behind such ends in order to enable the study of Hesse's means, making her means intelligible. They are the inevitable debris of the reckless act of experimentation, reclaimed and imbued with alchemical import.

This use of artistic test-pieces as a means (without end) recalls Avital Ronell's peculiar deployment of the "prototype" in her book *The Test Drive* (2007). In an attempt to understand—and ultimately deconstruct—the notion of the test, Ronell proposes a series of prototypes constituting different approaches to the practice of testing. These approaches range widely across disciplinary divides, including philosophical, scientific, and literary prototypes. What is unique about each prototype in Ronell's work is how they do not merely test hypotheses or contribute to a coherent "thesis" concerning the meaning and nature of testing. Rather, each prototype returns us to the very question of what testing consists of, or what contaminations are left out of any given scientific experiment. The net result of piling on these protocols is a constant reminder to return to the very potentiality of testability that is pliable enough to constantly produce new uses beyond any predetermined end.

Prototypes as test-pieces are not merely processes from which the artist or scientist can *learn* how to better accomplish a task or complete an experiment or improve as a professional or resolve a problem. Indeed, if there is an "outcome" to her own iterative prototype writing, it is, for Ronell, "stupidity" as the "experience of exposure without recourse to more reassuring types of evaluations" (75). Prototypes do not point toward a definitive conclusion, solution, evaluation. Another way of saying this might be that prototypes betray their ends (rather than merely point the way toward their ends), and therefore unleash a certain amount of experimental wandering or drift back toward the potentiality (the test drive, as Ronell calls it) that ends presuppose (yet ultimately exhaust). Such potentiality is not for the sake of completion (as with the prototype in a finite experiment) but rather offers a window into a nonfinite, recursive, drifting modality of testing. Test-pieces, therefore, would not be part of an economy of learning (that results in the transformation of nonknowledge into knowledge), and as such, cannot be considered works or acts of communication (beyond certain paradoxical formulations or states). Instead, they are unpractical, noneconomic, ritualistic processes that are disinterested in ends and point toward an investigation of means.

Rules for Protocol Writing

Protocols as a form of preparatory writing can produce certain anxieties in those who are suddenly adrift from the stability and familiarity of the lecture. It releases the professor or lecturer from the *work* of writing the lecture and separates "teaching" from the act of communication. But what remains of education when learning—as work and communication for *both* professor and student—are suspended? What then is made common, what is set in drift? In our first attempt to create a situation of and for studioing—a research happening we titled "Education as Experimentation: Possibilities beyond Outcome-Based Learning" (2017)—we invited participants to write short protocols to suspend the operative logic of learning (meaning, the ways in which the metaphysics of learning become operationalized in practice). To our surprise, participants struggled with this form of writing. Because of the unusual format, there was a sense of personal risk in appearing senseless or unprepared or unprofessional in front of peers. They had difficulty truly embracing the risk necessary for real experimentation and the kind of vulnerability and awkwardness it can induce. In short, they had not yet cultivated the necessary recklessness required for the endeavor—reckless in the sense of *indifference* to outcomes and ends (rather than mere carelessness). We had to reassure particular participants that such risk-taking was essential to the research happening as a whole. Also, other participants could not separate the protocol from an intended learning outcome. They had a hard time embracing the contingency and indeterminateness of the protocol once studious drift was set in motion. The gravitational pull of the lecture and learning were difficult to drift away from, and would often pull the protocol back into their orbit. Indeed, there seemed to be a sense that the conference would be considered a "failure" if the participants did not learn something they could take home to "improve" their pedagogy. Given these pressures, we produced the cryptogenealogy outlined previously from which we derived certain pataphysical principles and rules (rather than metaphysical laws of functionality):

Principles
1. Experimentation is ontologically primary. Use comes before function.
2. Experimentation necessitates the space and time of studioing.
3. Studioing sets adrift subjects, things, actions, discourses, and practices from within yet against the metaphysics of learning.
4. The educational logic of studioing is study as defined by rules for unproductive ritual (as a pure means rather than a means to an end as with works of communication).
5. The situation of studioing is anarchic because it lacks authority or sovereignty to determine its foundations or ends, value, meaning, or measure.

Rules for Protocol writing

1. Embrace an absurdist, paradoxical, parodic mindset that views awkwardness as generative.
2. Suspend, neutralize, and deactivate ideas, actions, and learning logics.
3. Introduce limited constraints or rules based on a minimalist aesthetic (nothing too complicated . . . only include what is *necessary* and *sufficient* to suspend, neutralize, and deactivate).
4. Write protocols that extend and intensify drift in terms of places, people, things, and ideas that can be incorporated into the experiment to produce thinking through mediatic displacements.
5. Make experimentation common. Be sure the protocol can be implemented with limited funds/resources so that the maximum number of human animals, nonhuman animals, things, and places can participate.
6. Be genuinely experimental, balancing formal constraints, open procedure, and chance and fortune. The idea here is not to confirm results based on an existing hypothesis but rather to see what happens when a protocol is collectively performed.

Where for Art Thou, University?

For essentially eight hundred years, the university's pedagogy has revolved around the writing and performing of lectures. Because of this history, it seems difficult to imagine a university that is not in some way wedded to or founded upon the lecture. This means that if the formal structure of the lecture is suspended then it signals either (a) the death of the university itself, or (b) the renewal of the university through more sophisticated pedagogical forms transcending the outdated and outmoded remnant of the lecture. We reject both of these options and instead want to *redeem* the movement animating the lecture by rendering inoperative the form of the lecture. The pataphysics of drift are not, therefore, the antithesis of the lecture so much as a parallel dimension within the lecture, an alternative educational universe that lies in wait and can be unlocked when the genealogy of the lecture is interrupted by the cryptogenealogy of books of secrets, impossible blueprints, and test-pieces. When this happens, the formal structures of the lecture and the lecture hall give way to the situation of studioing (as a contact between movements, bodies, and ideas). Yet studioing is not the antithesis of lecturing, but rather an intensification and extension of the kind of profanatory drift that the lecture sets in motion. By intensification we mean ultimately creating rules of use that challenge the authority of the text or the professor/lecturer or the institution, and by extension we mean the movement continues to give itself away to audiences and participants that lack institutional recognition and yet are capable of hacking into and tinkering with the technological infrastructure underlying the metaphysics of learning. This means making the secret rules of study common, ensuring that the pliable space-time machine of the studio is part of a commonwealth of practices and ideas.

In this sense, we must reimagine the professor/lecturer as a postdigital scyborg. For la paperson, the scyborg is a "reorganizer of institutional machinery" that "subverts machinery against the master code of its makers" (2017, 55) that makes another kind of university possible beyond the "first world" colonialist university (and, we might add, its educational metaphysics based on learning). The term "scyborg" is a rather monstrous (if not alchemical) contact between system and cyborg, reminding us that cyborgs are always plugged into complex social, institutional, political, and economic systems that they capitulate to and reproduce but also potentially reject and betray. Because of the position within yet against, the university scyborg can cobble together a third university out of infrastructural scraps of the first-world colonialist university.

In our view, part of the university scyborg's practice is the writing of protocols that (a) render inoperative educational metaphysics of economized learning to produce (b) situations of studioing. In this sense, protocol-writing engages in institutional piracy in order to intensify and expand studioing. Through this type of writing and its enactment in and against institutional structures, the scyborg embodies what Ronell would describe as the "personality of the experimenter" or the educational "daredevil" or "risk-taker" (2007, 217) who is wrapped up in "nonfinite experiments" (217) that cannot end (and who could not desire one). This personality lives within a "perpetual proving ground" (324) opened up by the risk-taking demanded by the prototype. Because of the uncertainty of such reckless risk-taking, the prototype indicates a "shriveling of authority" (205), as there is no expertise to guide the prototype or definitively evaluate its value or worth in terms of works or acts of communication. Without authority, the university scyborg is in perpetual threat of losing his or her professional status or value. Not unlike Professor Challenger, the university scyborg betrays the self (and the consistency of the self) in an act of drift. And yet there is an anarchic freedom that the scyborg is in a particular privileged position to make common and thus share with those who lack such privilege (both inside and outside institutional boundaries). Without authority, yet with access to the infrastructure of the first-world colonialist university, the scyborg as protocol-generating machine can invite others into the studio (or extend the studio out for others) for experimentation beyond learning.

The e-learning platform is currently emerging as a major form of university infrastructure that could come to define the horizon of the university. We cannot simply allow the media to overtake the thinking that the university form makes possible (browsing). Nor can we simply or easily impose the summiting of learning into the virtual sphere (transforming it into a classroom). Instead, we have to creatively use this infrastructure in such a way as to induce the drift of unpractical and ritualistic thinking through protocol-writing. It is our contention that digital technologies meant for e-learning can become a way to intensify and extend studious drift, becoming a means for virtualizing the studio as the space and time of an impossible institution: the pataphysical university composed of reckless scyborgs who are busy tinkering with secret recipes in order to give them away.

Conclusion: (D)rifting

WE END WITH a rather enigmatic portrait of studioing that will enable us to consider the broader political implications of the pataphysics of studious drift. In the short story titled "The New Advocate," Kafka tells of Bucephalus, who is a retired war horse that has taken up the study of the law. The last line of the story reads, "So perhaps it is really best to do as Bucephalus has done and absorb oneself in law books. In the quiet lamplight, his flanks unhampered by the thighs of a rider, free and far from the clamor of battle, he reads and turns the pages of our ancient tomes" (1971, 415). Drawing inspiration from Walter Benjamin's interpretation of this scene, Agamben argues that the gate to justice rests in the activity of deactivation (of the law). Summarizing this point, Agamben writes, "In the Kafka essay, the enigmatic image of a law that is studied but no longer practiced corresponds, as a sort of remnant, to the unmasking of mythico-juridical violence affected by pure violence. There is, therefore, still a possible figure of law after its nexus with violence and power has been deposed, but it is a law that no longer has force or application, like the one in which the 'new attorney,' leafing through 'our old books,' buries himself in study." (2005, 63).

Whereas learning (in schools and universities) takes place during the day, studying often takes place predominantly at night (precisely when we should be sleeping, preparing for the next day's lessons). It is therefore illicit and fugitive, happening where and when it should not. The studious practice of Bucephalus is displaced from any form of work or communication; he sits silent, free, and far from his function as a war machine, ritualistically flipping pages in a law that is no longer in force. This studier, in the suspended space-time of the studio, is an anarchic figure, somehow beyond the law yet without destroying the law. Indifferent to ends, he continues to ritualistically flip pages back and forth, searching through the law for secrets, finding harmonious discords.

On our reading, studioing is the temporalization and spatialization of the anarchy of study—the home to that which has no home within the metaphysics of learning that has come to define the university. By anarchy we do not mean chaos. Instead, as Bucephalus's example indicates, we mean a suspension of the law in order to experiment with forms of educational life that are ritualistic and unpractical. Bucephalus does not produce works that communicate. Instead, his life is defined by a fugitive practice with its own internal rules (secret recipes, protocols) for study. In this anarchic practice, the law is transformed into an object that Bucephalus plays with like an artistic test-object. The law has no active, living authority over Bucephalus. He lives a life that is ungovernable (by and through the enactment of law). It no longer gives commands, and in this sense can be read and interpreted *by anyone at any time*.

For Heidegger, as discussed in the introduction to this book, research in the university has become a form of technological enframing. To design an experiment is to set up a series of constraints, including a law (or laws) that hold over a certain set of objects. This law enables the researcher to stay on a path, evaluate outcomes, and (hopefully) predict future results. Embedded in this research model is the metaphysics of learning. Yet for Bucephalus, the law is no longer in force, it no longer controls what objects ought to be privileged, how they ought to be evaluated, and its attempt to control contingency through predictive modeling no longer operates. And for this reason, Bucephalus is able to study the law without a path, and thus take real risks that are unsupported by the law's authority.

Bucephalus is therefore not so much a researcher as an anarchic scyborg (both human and inhuman, both inside and outside the academic traditions of scholarship) recklessly playing with what makes itself possible in the wake of the law. Reckless, in this case, has two meanings. First, Bucephalus is not concerned with living up to the expectations of the law, nor is he interested in learning anything from the law (how to live an operative, effective, productive life according to its metaphysical principles, or how to predict the future according to calculated probabilities). He plays with the law in a generative way, opening it up for new, unknown, and as-of-yet undetermined uses that only emerge when the power of the law to regulate, define, and capture is neutralized. Second, he is reckless in the sense that study does not wreck anything. It does not destroy that which it takes up. Instead, the protocols that the studier follows and lives by are rendered inoperative through unpractical and noncommunicative ritual. This unpractical practice is reckless, meaning it is without violence, without damage. It is as anarchic as it is pacifistic.

In his book *The Art of Recklessness,* the poet Dean Young offers a useful analogy, "The poet is like one of those cartoon characters who has stepped off the cliff only to remain suspended. But while the cartoon character's realization of his irrational predicament brings about its fall, for the poet imagination sustains this reckless position over the abyss; it is what extends the view" (2010, 147–48). The studier is much like Young's poet hovering over the abyss, waiting to be set aloft/adrift by strange currents of ethernity. In this sense, the abyss is not empty, but rather full with a pataphysical overflow of ether that supports the poet's imagination to create impossible solutions (to the problem of "falling off a cliff"). In this example, the summiting learner is the one who falls, because she does not embrace imagination to abandon the laws of learnification. The imagination is also anarchic in so far as it is indifferent to realities and laws and provides access to ethernity. Imagination is a prerequisite for the practice of recklessness and studious drift. It negates laws without destroying them, opening up the parallel space of the studio, which can be conjured up at any place at any time. Thus the studier's reckless yet ritualistic study is not because she lacks imagination to escape. Rather, the anarchic dimension of the imagination is unleashed from functionality, diving into the drift of ethernity.

The risk of the studioing is an imaginative leap off the cliff that tethers education to the metaphysics of learning. In suspending the law, Bucephalus abandons himself to an educational life without measure. Thus the drift of studioing is not merely the endless circulation of learning and laboring found within the learning society. Nor is it the repetitive deconstruction of such circulation without escape, wherein the promise of education is always to come. Rather the ritualistic and unproductive drift found in the space and time of the studio is first and foremost a *rift* in the fabric of education and its economization under learning. (D)rifting sets up a parallel, pataphysical dimension within yet beyond what is presently possible, occupying the infrastructure of learning so as to neutralize its powers. An educational alchemy is possible here that produces a different, posthuman and postdigital body. When this esoteric (secret) practice becomes exoteric, when Bucephalus multiplies and spreads, then the anarchy of (d)rifting reveals its political possibilities as a collective concern. It has been our wager throughout this book that digital (d)rift is one way in which studioing can be made common, and in so doing, open up a new contact point between education and politics.

Let's then join Bucephalus to create a situation of e-studioing for a postpandemic world in which the space-time machine of the studio, the impractical practice of study, and reckless protocol-writing combine to intensify and extend common secrets by taking advantage of the pataphysics of postdigital (d)rift. In an imagined pataphysical university, the secret recipes for study written down by horses (and poets) would be made common through the dissemination of protocols. In this way, the studio as a virtual space-time machine fueled by ether would be encountered by a swarm of drifters (rather than occupied by lone studiers). Now is a time when the potentiality for such extension and intensification are palpable and can be pirated from the first-world colonialist university by scyborgs in order to make e-studioing possible. The anarchy of the studio and its pataphysics of study can be set adrift, and through the rift that is created, the educational use of ethernity can finally be explored by the multitude.

Acknowledgments

In our effort to conjure the imaginary solutions posited in these pages, we were aided and abetted by fellow adventurers in common experimentation. These include the participants of Studio_D, and especially the teams who contributed their protocols: Hu Jun and Christopher Moffett; xtine burrough and Sabrina Starnaman; Kim Lesley, Maya Pindyck, and Daniel Tucker; Sebastian Schlecht, Tomi Slotte Dufva, Taneli Tuovinen, Juuso Tervo, and Annika Sohlman; Cala Coats and David Tinapple; Joris Vlieghe and Nancy Vansieleghem; James Thurman; and Daniel Friedrich and Nathan Holbert. We're grateful to Kate Wurtzel for her meaningful reading of the book in its early stages. The Studio_D webpages were made possible by the expertise of Monica Scott. Kim Willis provided vital administrative support. We also thank the former leadership team of Greg Watts, Denise Baxter, and Eric Ligon in the College of Visual Arts and Design at the University of North Texas for their encouragement. Lastly, we thank the Onstead Foundation and C. Loren Vandiver for providing resources that allowed the Onstead Institute to realize Studio_D.

Bibliography

Agamben, Giorgio. 1993. *The Coming Community*. Translated by Michael Hardt. Minneapolis: University of Minnesota Press.

Agamben, Giorgio. 1995. *Idea of Prose*. Translated by Michael Sullivan and Sam Whitsitt. New York: SUNY Press.

Agamben, Giorgio. 2005. *State of Exception*. Translated by Kevin Attell. Chicago: University of Chicago Press.

Agamben, Giorgio. 2017. *Autoritratto nello Studio*. Milan: Luce Mediterranea.

Agamben, Giorgio. 2018. *What Is Real?* Translated by Lorenzo Chiesa. Stanford, Calif.: Stanford University Press.

Agamben, Giorgio. 2021. "Requiem per gli Studenti." Diario della Crisi, accessed February 15, 2021, https://www.iisf.it/index.php/attivita/ pubblicazioni-e-archivi/diario-della-crisi/giorgio-agamben-requiem-per-gli-studenti.html.

Ahmed, Sara. 2006. *Queer Phenomenology: Orientations, Objects, Others*. Durham, N.C.: Duke University Press.

Algazi, Gadi. 2012. "At the Study: Notes on the Production of the Scholarly Self." In *Space and Self in Early Modern European Cultures,* edited by David Warren Sabean and Malina Stefanovska, 17–50. Toronto: University of Toronto Press.

Aronowitz, Stanley. 2001. *The Knowledge Factory: Dismantling the Corporate University and Creating True Higher Learning*. Boston: Beacon Press.

Arsenjuk, Luka, and Michelle Koerner. 2009. "Study, Students, Universities: An Introduction." *Polygraph* 21:1–13.

Bayne, Siân, Peter Evans, Rory Ewins, Jeremy Knox, James Lamb, Hamish McLeod, Clara O'Shea, Jen Ross, Philippa Sheail, and Christine Sinclair. 2020. *The Manifesto for Teaching Online*. Cambridge, Mass.: MIT Press.

Benjamin, Walter. 2012. *The Correspondence of Walter Benjamin, 1910–1940*. Translated by Manfred R. Jacobson and Evelyn M. Jacobson. Chicago: University of Chicago Press.

Biesta, Gert J. J. 2006. *Beyond Learning: Democratic Education for a Human Future*. New York: Routledge.

Cole, Michael, and Mary Pardo. 2005. "Origins of the Studio." In *Inventions of the Studio, Renaissance to Romanticism,* edited by Michael Cole and Mary Pardo, 1–35. Chapel Hill: University of North Carolina Press.

Debord, Guy. 2006. "A User's Guide to Détournement." In *Situationist International: Anthology,* translated by Ken Knabb, 14–20. Berkeley: Bureau of Public Secrets.

Deleuze, Gilles. 1995a. *Difference and Repetition*. Translated by Paul Patton. New York: Columbia University Press.

Deleuze, Gilles. 1995b. *Negotiations*. Translated by Martin Joughin. New York: Columbia University Press.

Deleuze, Gilles. 2007. "What Is a Creative Act?" In *Two Regimes of Madness: Texts and Interviews, 1975–1995,* translated by David Lapoujade, 312–24. Los Angeles: Semiotext(e).

Deleuze, Gilles, and Felix Guattari. 1986. *Kafka: Toward a Minor Literature*. Translated by Dana Polan. Minneapolis: University of Minnesota Press.

Deleuze, Gilles, and Felix Guattari. 1987. *A Thousand Plateaus: Capitalism and Schizophrenia*. Translated by Brian Massumi. Minneapolis: University of Minnesota Press.

Deleuze, Gilles, and Claire Parnet. 1996. *Dialogues*. Translated by Hugh Tomlinson and Barbara Habberjam. New York: Columbia University Press.

Drucker, Johanna. 2009. *SpecLab: Digital Aesthetics and Projects in Speculative Computing*. Chicago: University of Chicago Press.

Eamon, William. 1994. *Science and the Secrets of Nature: Books of Secrets in Medieval and Early Modern Culture*. Princeton, N.J.: Princeton University Press.

Eisenstein, Elizabeth L. 1997. *The Printing Press as an Agent of Change: Communications and Cultural Transformations in Early-Modern Europe*. Cambridge: Cambridge University Press.

Fabricant, Michael, and Stephen Brier. 2016. *Austerity Blues: Fighting for the Soul of Public Higher Education*. Baltimore, Md.: John Hopkins University Press.

Fer, Briony. 2004. *The Infinite Line: Remaking Art after Modernism*. London: Yale University Press.

Fisher, Ben. 2001. *Pataphysician's Library: An Exploration of Alfred Jarry's 'Livres pairs.'* Liverpool: Liverpool University Press.

Flusser, Vilém. 2014. *Gestures*. Translated by Nancy Ann Roth. Minneapolis: University of Minnesota Press.

Ford, Derek R. 2016. *Communist Study: Education for the Commons*. Lanham, Md.: Lexington Books.

Friesen, Norm. 2011. "The Lecture as Transmedial Pedagogical Form." *Educational Researcher* 40, no. 3: 95–102.

Giroux, Henry. 2007. *The University in Chains: Confronting the Military-Industrial-Academic Complex*. New York: Routledge.

Giroux, Henry, and Susan Searls Giroux. 2004. *Take Back Higher Education: Race, Youth, and the Crisis of Democracy in the Post-Civil Rights Era*. London: Palgrave Macmillan.

Harney, Stefano, and Fred Moten. 2013. *The Undercommons: Fugitive Planning and Black Study*. Brooklyn: Autonomedia.

Heidegger, Martin. 1977. "The Age of the World Picture." In *The Question Concerning Technology and Other Essays,* translated by William Lovitt, 115–54. New York: Harper Perennial.

Heidegger, Martin. 2002. *Identity and Difference*. Translated by Joan Stambaugh. Chicago: University of Chicago Press.

Horn, Michael B., and Heather Staker. 2014. *Blended: Using Disruptive Innovation to Improve Schools*. San Francisco: Jossey-Bass.

Hugill, Andrew. 2015. '*Pataphysics: A Useless Guide*. Cambridge, Mass.: MIT Press.

Jarry, Alfred. 1996. *Exploits & Opinions of Dr. Faustroll, Pataphysician*. Translated by Simon Watson Taylor. Cambridge, Mass.: Exact Change.

Jarry, Alfred. 2013. *How to Construct a Time Machine*. Translated by Roger Shattuck. Patakosmos Press.

Jones, Caitlin. 2010. "The Function of the Studio (When the Studio Is a Laptop)." *Artlies* 67 (Fall/Winter). https://faa218.files.wordpress.com/2014/08/jones_caitlin.pdf.

Jones, Caroline. 1996. *Machine in the Studio: Constructing the Postwar American Artist*. Chicago: University of Chicago Press.

Kafka, Franz. 1971. "The New Advocate." In *The Complete Stories,* translated by Willa and Edwin Muir, 414–15. New York: Shocken Books.

Kemp, Martin. 1995. "'Wrought by No Artist's Hand': The Natural, the Artificial, the Exotic, and the Scientific in Some Artifacts from the Renaissance." In *Reframing the Renaissance: Visual Culture in Europe and Latin America, 1450–1650,* edited by Claire Farago, 177–96. New Haven: Yale University Press.

la paperson. 2017. *A Third University Is Possible*. Minneapolis: University of Minnesota Press.

Laurillard, Diana. 2002. *Rethinking University Teaching: A Framework for the Effective Use of Educational Technology*. London: Routledge.

Lewis, Tyson E. 2013. *On Study: Giorgio Agamben and Educational Potentiality*. London: Routledge.

Lewis, Tyson E. 2017. *Inoperative Learning: A Radical Rewriting of Educational Potentialities*. New York: Routledge.

Lewis, Tyson E. 2019. "Studying: A Disinterested Passion." In *Keywords in Radical Philosophy and Education: Common Concepts for Contemporary Movements,* edited by Derek Ford, 398–407. Leiden: Brill.

Lewis, Tyson E. 2020. "The Pataphysics of Inoperativity in the Works of Giorgio Agamben." *Journal of Italian Philosophy* 3:139–61.

Lewis, Tyson E., and Samira Alirezabeigi. 2018. "Studying with the Internet: Giorgio Agamben, Education, and New Digital Technologies." *Studies in Philosophy and Education* 37: 553–66.

Lewis, Tyson E., and Daniel Friedrich. 2016. "Educational States of Suspension." *Educational Philosophy and Theory* 48, no. 3: 237–50.

Liberman, Alexander. 1960. *The Artist in His Studio*. New York: Viking Press.

Long, Phil, and George Siemens. 2011. "Penetrating the Fog: Analytics in Learning and Education." *Educause Review* 46, no. 5: 31–40.

Marin, Lavinia. 2020. *On the Possibility of a Digital University: Thinking and Mediatic Displacement at the University*. Cham, Switzerland: Springer.

Marin, Lavinia, Jan Masschelein, and Maarten Simons. 2018. "Page, Text, and Screen in the University: Revisiting the Illich Hypothesis." *Educational Philosophy and Theory* 50, no. 1: 49–60.

Masschelein, Jan, and Maarten Simons. 2008. "The Governmentalization of Learning and the Assemblage of a Learning Apparatus." *Educational Theory* 58, no. 4: 391–415.

Masschelein, Jan, and Maarten Simons. 2009. "Toward the Idea of a World University." *Interchange* 40:1–23.

Masschelein, Jan, and Maarten Simons. 2011. "*Universitas Magistrorum et Scholarium*: A Short History of Profanation." In *Curating the European University: Exposition and Public Debate,* edited by Maarten Simons, et al., 81–88. Leuven, Belgium: Leuven University Press.

Masschelein, Jan, and Maarten Simons. 2013. "The Politics of the University: Movements of (De-)Identification and the Invention of Public Pedagogic Forms." In *Education and the Political: New Theoretical Articulations,* edited by Tomasz Szkudlarek, 107–99. Rotterdam: Sense.

Masschelein, Jan, Maarten Simons, Ulrich Bröckling, and Ludwig Pongratz. 2007. *The Learning Society from the Perspective of Governmentality*. Hoboken, N.J.: Wiley-Blackwell.

Meyerhoff, Eli. 2019. *Beyond Education: Radical Studying for Another World*. Minneapolis: University of Minnesota Press.

Molderings, Herbert. 2007. "It is Not the Object That Counts, but the Experiments: Marcel Duchamp's New York Studio as a Laboratory of Perception." In *Re-Objects: Marcel Duchamp, Damien Hirst, Jeff Koons, Gerhard Merz,* edited by Eckhard Schneider, 35–51. Bregenz: Kunsthaus Bregenz.

Mytkowska, Joanna, and Andrzej Prywara. 2004. "Edward Krasinski's Studio." In *Who if not We Should at Least Try to Imagine the Future of All This?,* edited by Maria Hlavajova and Jill Winder, 128–45. Amsterdam: Artimo.

Noble, Safiya Umoja. 2018. *Algorithms of Oppression: How Search Engines Reinforce Racism*. New York: New York University Press.

O'Doherty, Brian. 2007. *Studio and Cube*. Princeton, N.J.: Princeton Architectural Press.

Praz, Mario. 1975. *Studies in Seventeenth-Century Imagery*. Rome: Storia e Letteratura.

Principe, Lawrence M. 2013. *The Secrets of Alchemy*. Chicago: University of Chicago Press.

Rasmi, Jacopo, and Hans Schildermans, eds. 2021. *Ecologies of Study: A Book of Secrets*. Saint-Étienne: Unité de Recherche ECLLA.

Readings, Bill. 1997. *The University in Ruins*. Cambridge, Mass.: Harvard University Press.

Renner, Eric. 2004. *Pinhole Photography, Third Edition: Rediscovering a Historic Technique*. Waltham, Mass.: Focal Press.

Ronell, Avital. 2007. *The Test Drive*. Chicago: University of Illinois Press.

Ryberg, Thomas. 2021. "Postdigital Research, Networked Learning, and COVID-19." *Postdigital Science and Education* 3:266–71.https://doi.org/10.1007/s42438-021-00223-x.

Selmi, Elisabetta. 2008. *Le stanze segrete: Le donne Bresciane si revelando*. 2008. Brescia: Fondazione Civiltà Bresciana.

Shattock, Roger. 1960. "Superliminal Note." *Evergreen Review* 4, no. 13: 23–33.

Slaughter, Sheila, and Gary Rhoades. 2009. *Academic Capitalism and the New Economy*. Baltimore, Md.: Johns Hopkins University Press.

Thornton, Dora. 1998. *The Scholar in His Study: Ownership and Experience in Renaissance Italy*. London: Yale University Press.

Vlieghe, Joris. 2017. "Education in an Age of Digital Technologies: Flusser, Stiegler, and Agamben on the Idea of the Posthistorical." *Philosophy and Technology* 27, no. 4: 519–37.

Webb, Dianna. 2007. *Privacy and Solitude: The Medieval Discovery of Personal Space*. London: Bloomsbury.

Wood, Christopher S. 2005. "Indoor-Outdoor: The Studio around 1500." In *Inventions of the Studio, Renaissance to Romanticisme,* edited by Michael Cole and Mary Pardo, 36–72. Chapel Hill: University of North Carolina Press.

Young, Dean. 2010. *The Art of Recklessness: Poetry as Assertive Force and Contradiction*. Minneapolis: Greywolf Press.

Zarrilli, Phillip. 2002. "The Metaphysical Studio." *Drama Review* 46, no. 2: 157–70.

Zhao, Weili. 2019. "Daoist Onto-Un-Learning as a Radical Form of Study: Re-Imagining Learning and Study from an Eastern Perspective." *Studies in Philosophy and Education* 38, no. 3: 261–73.

(Continued from page iii)

Forerunners: Ideas First

Tyson E. Lewis is professor of art education in the College of Visual Arts and Design at the University of North Texas. His books include *Walter Benjamin's Anti-fascist Education: From Riddles to Radio*.

Peter B. Hyland is director of the Jo Ann (Jody) and Dr. Charles O. Onstead Institute for Education in the Visual Arts and Design at the University of North Texas and author of the poetry collection *Out Loud*.